DOING THEOLOGY
IN AN EVOLUTIONARY WAY

Contents

Introduction.....................................ix

Part One:
The Inherited Theological Landscape

1. What Is Theology? 3
    Faith Seeking Understanding....................4
    Contextual Understanding in the
        Twenty-First Century......................6
    New Scientific Wisdom.......................9
    The Evolutionary Imperative..................13
    Theology, Old and New......................15
    A Spirit-Evolving God.......................19

2. The Codependent Paradigm..................23
    The Anthropocentric Deviation.................25
    The Flawed Creation.........................28
    The Fall and Redemption.....................29
    From Paul Back to Jesus.....................33
    Beyond the Disempowering Cross..............37
    Let the Paradigm Die!.......................41

3. The Imperial Judeo-Christian Paradigm..........43
    Creation: God's Own Starting Point........., ...44
    Israel as Symbol ..,, ...46
    Israel and Jesus...........................48
    Enter the Church...........................50

DOING THEOLOGY IN AN EVOLUTIONARY WAY

❧

Diarmuid O'Murchu, MSC

ORBIS BOOKS
www.orbisbooks.com

ORBIS BOOKS
www.orbisbooks.com

Fathers and Brothers MARYKNOLL

Founded in 1970, Orbis Books endeavors to publish works that enlighten the mind, nourish the spirit, and challenge the conscience. The publishing arm of the Maryknoll Fathers and Brothers, Orbis seeks to explore the global dimensions of the Christian faith and mission, to invite dialogue with diverse cultures and religious traditions, and to serve the cause of reconciliation and peace. The books published reflect the views of their authors and do not represent the official position of the Maryknoll Society. To learn more about Maryknoll and Orbis Books, please visit our website at www.maryknollsociety.org.

Manufactured in the United States of America

Library of Congress Cataloging-in-Publication Data

Names: O'Murchu, Diarmuid, author.
Title: Doing theology in an evolutionary way / Diarmuid O'Murchu.
Description: Maryknoll, NY: Orbis Books, [2021] | Includes bibliographical references and index.
Identifiers: LCCN 2020031304 (print) | LCCN 2020031305 (ebook) | ISBN 9781626984042 (print) | ISBN 9781608338689 (ebook)
Subjects: LCSH: Theology—History—21st century. | Creation. | Evolution—Religious aspects—Christianity.
Classification: LCC BT28 .O17 2021 (print) | LCC BT28 (ebook) | DDC 230/.2 dc23
LC record available at https://lccn.loc.gov/2020031304
LC ebook record available at https://lccn.loc.gov/2020031305

Clericalized Power 51
Popular Devotion 53
Heresy and Monolithic Truth 54
Incarnational Altruism 56
Eschatology: Disillusion or Fulfillment 57

4. Progressive Christianity:
Beyond Clericalized Theology 59
The Progressive Option 61
The Clerical Shift 64
Faith Community Reconfigured 67
The Christian Focus 69

**Part Two:
Theological Horizons of the Twenty-First Century**

5. Theology's Paschal Journey:
The Paradoxical Imperative 77
The Paradoxical Imperative 80
We Are the Sixth Extinction 84
Christ's Death and Resurrection 87
Religion's Paschal Journey 93
Continuity and Tradition 95

6. The Originating Spirit 99
Out of the Depths 101
The Spirit in Genesis 104
Spirit and the Creative Vacuum 108
All Is Energy 112
Meaning from Within 114
Spirit Will Not Be Bound! 117

7. Creation as Embodied Birthing 119
The Body and Embodiment 120
Creative Birthing 123
Bringing Jesus to Birth 125
And the Birthing Continues 128
Healing the Wounded Body 130
Birthing in the Power of Sexuality 135

   Birthing Empowerment 139
8. The Evolutionary Imperative 141
   Conceptual Clarity 142
   New Horizons 145
      The Spell of Solidity 145
      Sense of Direction 146
      Driven by Consciousness 148
      Imbued with Paradox 149
      Lateral Thinking 150
      Cooperation 152
   Beyond the Religious-Scientific Collusion 154
   The Anthropological Shift 156
   The Trinity in Evolutionary Context 158
   Faith in an Evolutionary God 161
9. Empowering Incarnation 163
   Whither Deep Incarnation? 164
   Embodiment Reenvisioned 168
      Relational Identity 171
      The Sensuous Body 172
      Transhuman Embodiment 172
   Interreligious Grounding 173
   Dislodging the Postcolonial Baggage 176
   Letting Go for Letting Be 180
   Toward an Incarnational Church 183
   Theological Embodiment 185
10. When Theology Embraces Spirituality 187
   Spirituality and Consciousness 189
   People of the Story 191
   Changing Worldviews 192
   Spirituality Informing Theology 194
   Toward a More Integrated Spirituality 197
   Conclusion 201

Bibliography 203

Index 215

Introduction

In the course of the twentieth century, theology underwent a massive paradigm shift. Only now, as we move deeper into the twenty-first century, are the contours becoming clear, and as yet, the implications are largely unexplored. How the shift can be named and explained will largely depend on the context out of which the interpreter is operating. But it is also dependent on cosmic and planetary forces that today inform human consciousness to a degree unknown in previous times. These new contextual horizons include enlarged scientific understandings of cosmology and anthropology, evolutionary unfolding, quantum physics, consciousness-awareness, globalization, cultural diversity, and postmodernism.

As Karl Rahner hinted at many years ago, the Christian of the future will be a mystic or will not be at all; this applies even more forcibly to the emerging theology of our time, bearing in mind that mysticism celebrates, above all else, the enduring *oneness* evidenced throughout creation. The contemporary theologian will be a multidisciplinary visionary or won't be at all. If theology is the science of pursuing ultimate meaning (according to Paul Tillich), today that new horizon requires familiarity with several different disciplines, and needs to transcend the time-honored distinction between the sacred and the secular.

Three theological paradigms are under review in this book. The first two belong to the confessional tradition, Christian in nature and supporting faith in Jesus as the Christ, the source of our salvation. The third embraces a new sense of God at work, primarily in creation, and laterally in human beings. Celebration of evolutionary life, rather than salvation for humans, is the newly emerging horizon. Coming to the fore is the God who works in and through creation, rather than Jesus and the Christian narrative. As in contemporary theopoetics, the *logos* of *Theos* is shifting from an anthropocentric to a cosmic focus.

The first I name as *codependent paradigm*, described simply as Creation–Fall–Redemption. The central emphasis here is on the flawed nature of everything in creation. Although it is God's creation, God cannot rectify the fall, attributed to human recklessness (an irrational craving for power), so Jesus is missioned to rescue the flawed reality, a task that continues in the life of the church, often ensuing in humans entangled in several codependent relationships—hence, a primary reason why humans, maturing into a more adult consciousness, walk away from such an unhealthy faith system.

The second landscape I name as the *imperial Judeo-Christian paradigm*, which runs like this: Creation–Israel–Jesus–Church–Eschaton. More central to this paradigm is the rescuing imperial God of the Hebrew Scriptures, modeled primarily on the great King David, who in turn becomes the paradigmatic model for Jesus as Messiah. That same kingly, royal imperative permeates Christianity up to our own time. Although vehemently denounced and opposed by Jesus—as argued throughout this book—Constantine reestablished the imperial prerogative that then morphed into popes, bishops, and exclusive male clergy, with accompanying institutions to uphold patriarchal power. Of course, it will never truly satisfy authentic spiritual desire, in which case we need the eschatological clause assuring us that God will eventually bring the whole thing to an end in a final act of divine deliverance.

The third landscape is postconfessional and has a radically different feel to it; even the language will initially seem strange. I name it as the *evolutionary paradigm*. It goes like this: Spirit–Energy–Creation–Evolution–Incarnation–Spirituality. Looks like we have dropped the very word, *God*! No explicit reference to Father, Jesus, or Holy Spirit, but fret not, they are included. No allusion to fall, redemption, church, or eschaton. And the reader may already be wondering what has happened to revelation, and to the inspiration of sacred Scripture. On top of all that, this paradigm looks rather impersonal!

The myth of origin is crucial here, as indeed it is for every faith system. Beyond the ex-nihilo prerogative of the patriarchal male creator lies a more ancient creative energy, insinuating the dark deep out of which the Great Spirit energizes all life—*ex profundis*. The Great Spirit is how indigenous peoples around our world name the divine reality (God). Energized by the Great Spirit, the Birthing Holy One begets the vast panorama we call *creation*, setting in motion the irreversible complex trajectory that today we call *evolution*. The evolving creative enterprise eventually gives birth to (incarnates) consciously embodied creatures called *humans*, for whom the historical Jesus serves as an archetypal model. Finally, I am suggesting that our primary theological responsibility at this time is to name and celebrate that magnificent mythopoetic drama within an empowering spirituality for our age.

Without church, hierarchy, or formalized religion, this evolutionary paradigm inhabits an open-ended theological landscape, unashamedly postmodern, wild, transgressive, and scary, with the proverbial mix of peril and promise. However, it has hope inscribed deep within it, and in that, more than anything else, rests its credibility and authenticity.

Part One

The Inherited Theological Landscape

Prior to the twentieth century, theology could be described as sacred learning par excellence. Its subject material was the mystery of God and the divine presence uniquely embodied in the church. The word was first used by Plato to describe philosophical discourse on God,[1] quite similar to Augustine's description as reasoning or discussion concerning the Deity. In the Latin tradition, theology became identified with the rational study of the doctrines of the Christian religion, using Scripture as the deposit of revealed truth. Often described as "The Queen of the Sciences" in the high Middle Ages, theology served as the capstone for all serious academic study. Such a preeminent status was not seriously challenged until the Enlightenment in the eighteenth century.

---

[1] See Plato in *The Republic* II.18. Aristotle divided theoretical philosophy into mathematics, physics, and theology. In his schema, theology corresponds closely to metaphysics, which, for Aristotle, included discourse on the nature of the divine. The Latin author Boethius writing in the early sixth century, used *theologia* to denote a subdivision of philosophy as a subject of academic study, dealing with the motionless, incorporeal, divine reality.

1

Traditionally, Christian theology concentrates on the texts of the Old and New Testaments as well as on Christian tradition. Christian theologians use biblical exegesis, rational analysis, and argument to promote and uphold a deeper understanding of how God works in the world, and specifically in the life of the Church, wherein the bishops are understood to be the primary guardians of theological truth. In the past two centuries Christian theologians have become increasingly self-critical about how theology is done, especially regarding sources and procedures.

Central to the inherited theological paradigm is the all-powerful and all-knowing ruling God, the primary source of revealed truth as outlined in Holy Scripture. This God is understood to rule through the patriarchal, hierarchical line, favoring males over females, Roman imperial knowledge over universal wisdom, and theological truth as developed in the Christian Church. Within this context, male clerics have long been regarded as the exemplary candidates for theological wisdom and, in the Catholic Church after the Council of Trent (1545–1563), the sole beneficiaries of theological learning (until the mid-twentieth century).

Also central to the inherited theological paradigm was the view of the human as innately sinful, requiring an act of divine rescue, considered to be necessary for all people, and not merely for Christians. And in all cases, only Jesus of Nazareth could deliver such salvation. In essence theology was reduced to soteriology, and the divine creativity at work throughout creation was eclipsed by a perverse anthropology, in which the human came to be seen as superior to everything else in God's creation.

We are dealing with a closed system in which the ruling God requires ruling males, especially clerics, to help rope in the wayward humans, trusting that they will obey, so that they can save their immortal souls. Control and fear dominate the theological landscape, subverting the empowering liberation promised in the name of the Christian gospel. This model (paradigm) continues to flourish in several evangelical contexts, but when people become more self-aware and intellectually critical, it begins to fragment and is likely to be in substantial disarray by the end of the twenty-first century.

What Is Theology?

It is no longer about being correct. It is about being connected.

Richard Rohr

Theologies of creation have followed the orders of various orthodoxies and run almost dry.

Catherine Keller

In its Christian context, theology has had a two-pronged historical development. Particularly in the case of the Catholic Church, it belongs primarily to the teaching authority of the Church (often referred to as the magisterium). The promotion and protection of theological truth belongs primarily to the pope and is understood to be transmitted down through the various layers of the hierarchy, mainly through the bishops.

Second, theology belongs uniquely to a group of scholars known as theologians. In the past, they were selected and mandated by Church authority, and were chosen not merely for intellectual acumen but also for outstanding holiness. Their task was to unravel the mystery of God and God's relationship with our world, particularly with human beings. They followed a template, popularly known as revelation, divulging truths about the nature and meaning of God. The template was based on two foundations: Scripture and Tradition.

Scripture consists of both the Old and New Testaments, often referred to today as the First and Second Testaments. For much of Christian history Scripture was accessed through the Latin Bible—the Vulgate—translated by St. Jerome. It seems to have been taken largely at its face value and interpreted literally.

Tradition may be described as the work of the ancient Church Fathers, who attempted to translate into practical living the truths arising from revelation. Many of these truths were refined, and redefined, in Church synods and through papal teachings at various times in history. Not, however, until the nineteenth century (July 1870) did the infallibility of the pope evolve, whereby solemn papal pronouncements were to be heard and accepted as the word of the Godhead itself, and therefore deemed to be free of error.[1]

For much of Christian history, the scholars (theologians) helped the bishops determine how best to communicate truth to the people of God and the most effective catechetical methods to do so. Not until the twentieth century did we witness divergent views arising, as scholars often surfaced new insights from sources of which many bishops were only vaguely aware. Today, that gap grows ever wider as theology itself is evolving into a multidisciplinary science, accountable not so much to Church authority but rather to the growing body of spiritual searchers and seekers from multiple religious and secular backgrounds.

Faith Seeking Understanding

St. Anselm of Canterbury (1033–1109) was the first to define theology as *faith seeking understanding*, an approach adopted and advanced by St. Thomas Aquinas in the Middle Ages. In this

---

[1] Although papal infallibility was not definitively defined until 1870, the doctrine of Mary's Immaculate Conception, made by Pius IX in 1854, is considered an *ex cathedra* doctrine, as is her Assumption into heaven, made by Pius XII in 1950.

definition faith is understood as the deposit of faith, namely Scripture and Tradition. Such faith consisted in God-given truths that could never be altered. The teaching authority of the church (in the Catholic context, the magisterium) considered itself to be the guardian of unalterable truths, entrusted with the task of protecting the people of God from doctrinal error and misleading ideas.

Seeking understanding, therefore, denotes the unraveling of the meaning of Scripture itself and of the various church doctrines that comprised the tradition. The content was deemed unalterable, but the meaning, and its application to various different situations, required a range of possible understandings. This is where the Scripture scholar and theologian made a contribution.

The scholars, therefore, fulfilled a double role. First, they were teachers of the faith, a task that for most of Christian history largely belonged to seminaries in which young men were prepared for priesthood. Such teaching also took place in denominational universities, where most of the recipients were either preparing for, or already involved in, church ministry. Second, the theologians advised the bishops on matters of faith and morals. To what extent this actually happened is difficult to ascertain. Certainly, for the latter half of the twentieth century, quite a degree of tension prevailed between bishops and theologians.

In the Catholic Church a significant breakthrough happened in 1943, when Pope Pius XII issued a document titled *Divino Afflante Spiritu*, the subtitle of which is often translated: "On the Most Opportune Way to Pursue Biblical Studies." In this document, the pope is asking Catholic Scripture scholars not to rely solely on the Vulgate (the Latin Bible), but to also engage the ancient languages of Greek, Hebrew, and Aramaic. Effectively, the pope was requesting that literal interpretation of the Latin Bible should be superseded in favor of a deeper and more discerning analysis, arising from a more comprehensive acquaintance with older literary and cultural sources. American Catholic scholar Raymond Brown (1928–1998) described this document as the Magna Carta of Catholic biblical studies in the twentieth century.

From 1950 onward, thanks in part to the new guidelines issued by Pope Pius XII, the study of both Scripture and theology began to move in a new direction. Faith seeking understanding was seen in a new light. The very foundations of the faith itself were no longer perceived to be static and monolithic. New strategies of understanding—how to engage with ancient texts—were invoked. Truth came to be seen as an ongoing process and not merely as a once-and-for-all deposit.

Already by the 1960s, Scripture scholars and theologians were importing insights from other disciplines, notably ancient history and archaeology. (A minority had already been doing this since the late 1800s.) Nonclerical scholars began to play a more prominent role, and with their inclusion the former passive role of the laity began to shift. Various translations of the Bible were issued in languages that would encourage and support a wider lay readership.

Anselm's notion of faith seeking understanding took on quite a different meaning. The faith itself is rapidly outgrowing its confessional context, moving beyond the former limit of one truth only. More significantly, people are raising a range of new questions requiring diverse and novel responses. With the information explosion (from 1960 forward), the questing and questioning became ever more extensive. To the powers that be, nothing felt sacred anymore. In other words, their privileged protection of truth had been transcended by a new and different search for truth. The pursuit continues to our own day.

Contextual Understanding in the Twenty-First Century

Few can deny that the pace of change in the twenty-first century moves with ever greater rapidity. Most people experience it through ever frequent adjustments in areas as diverse as technology, working conditions, multiculturalism, globalization, political confusion, fashions, and climate change. Confronted with such changes, fewer people look to religion to help make sense of what is transpiring. This may be due, in part, to the fact that the formal religions themselves tend to react negatively to such rapid change.

At this juncture, religion and theology veer off in different directions. While religion tends to resent change, holding to its confessional allegiance—with the ever-growing body of lay theologians today—we encounter a new theological awakening. In the Catholic context, Jesuit Francis X. Clooney (2010) has long been pursuing a new comparative theology, embracing specifically the wisdom of the other great religions. Jerry L. Martin (2019) goes considerably further, aiming at a "theology without walls" that interfaces with a range of current issues. And with this openness and receptivity, theology is once more poised to become the queen of the sciences.

The emerging theological consciousness marks a response to three critical developments of the twenty-first century:

- Postcolonialism
- New scientific wisdom
- The evolutionary imperative of our time

Colonial influence in Christian history is often traced back to the Roman emperor Constantine (272–337), who in the fourth century paved the way for the acceptance and integration of Christianity as the official religion of the Roman Empire. After Constantine, the identification of God's will for humanity with the wishes of imperial force became endemic to the development of Christian faith. This imperial imperative dominated the theological landscape until the mid-twentieth century. Most Christian historians—and theologians—were born out of the culture of Christian imperialism. Theology was co-opted into the support and affirmation of the prevailing imperial power.

One contemporary field of study seeking to redress the preoccupation with such doctrinal colonization is that of *postcolonialism*. It moves in the direction of a double resolution. It seeks to highlight the complex nature of how power evolves and becomes insinuated in dominant modes of behavior, beyond the simplistic divide of winners and losers, victims and oppressors. It also unravels the messy nature of power-mongering, highlighting shifting alliances and complicit collusions, even to the point of the oppressed profiting from their own oppression. Postcolonialism may be described as a strategy for raising consciousness, sharpening our awareness, and refining our capacity for critical engagement with life and culture (more in O'Murchu 2014).

Postcolonial thinkers recognize that many of the assumptions that underlie the "logic" of colonialism are still active forces today. Thus, people's acceptance of, and allegiance to, inherited truths can often be in collusion with imperial values that have long outlived their usefulness and thus hinder people from progressing in more empowering ways. Influenced by advertising and powerful propaganda, black people may seek to emulate the values and behaviors of white Westerners, but this often-subconscious influence may be due to a deeply ingrained, collusive admiration left over from an earlier colonial epoch. This is what the postcolonialists name as the *residue*, which often translates into internalized oppression.

Over several centuries, women internalized the passivity imposed by patriarchal expectation. Aristotle's infamous allegation that females are effectively misbegotten males still underlies the inferior status of women in several major religions, Christianity included. Oppressed peoples often seek excessive attention and recognition because of internalized disregard left over from earlier slavery and oppression. At a more personal level, suppressed childhood abuse—sexual or otherwise—undermines authentic adult development, possibly for an entire lifetime. Internalized oppression pervades contemporary culture and may be most subtle of all in those nations and cultures that consider themselves to be developed and advanced. (For more on internalized oppression, see David 2013; O'Murchu 2014.)

The critical consciousness of our time—as illuminated through the postcolonial focus—detects in religion generally a psychological codependency (throwing one's life at the mercy of God), strong allegiance to patriarchal authority (emphasizing submission and passivity), and political posturing, using religion as a tool to dominate and control. Confronted with these residual elements, contemporary theologians feel an ever stronger and clearer mandate to illuminate the inherited baggage of internalized oppression, to expose the ecclesiastical and clerical collusions with imperial power, and to proffer an alternative empowering vision promising liberation and new hope. In the Christian context, this effectively means a radical reclamation of the gospel vision of the new reign of God.

Empowerment, therefore, becomes the central focus for the theological revival outlined in the present work. We seek to name more clearly the inherited power dynamics that are no longer useful, and therefore need to be replaced with a vision and set of strategies more conducive to growth and creativity. The context also changes, from that of humans as a superior species to an inclusion of all the other beings who share the web of life with us, including planet Earth and the cosmos at large. And the God who theologizes in and through all life-forms is no longer the imperial, fatherlike Creator, but the energizing Spirit who forever draws forth empowering possibilities to enhance and enrich our evolving creation. These new namings and the ensuing challenges are elucidated at greater length throughout this book.

New Scientific Wisdom

In the amorphous spiritual consciousness of our time (see Johnson and Ord 2012)—with many claiming to be spiritual but not religious—the scientific breakthroughs of the twentieth century are pushing theologians into ever more expansive horizons. One pertinent example is that of the papal encyclical of Pope Francis, *Laudato Si'* (published in 2015); such a Roman document, with its integrated blend of theology, ecology, and eco-justice, would have been inconceivable in twentieth-century

Catholicism. Two new scientific horizons have come into view: the new cosmology and the worldview embedded in quantum mechanics.

Several readers (especially within the United States) are already likely to be familiar with the new cosmology (sometimes described as the New Story). Texts such as *The Universe Story* (Swimme and Berry 1992), *Journey of the Universe* (Swimme and Tucker 2011), and *Radical Amazement* (Cannato 2006) provide valuable introductions. Despite some expansive views of creation in the Middle Ages, for most of its two-thousand-year history, Christianity viewed creation as a transitory, unreliable, problematic, sinful reality that would come to a cataclysmic end, yielding pride of place to the eternal glory of life hereafter. The universe, therefore, was viewed along lines quite similar to classical science: a mechanistic structure constituting isolated parts within a closed system, forever sliding down an entropic slope until it would eventually burn itself out; in the interim, it retained a practical value as a material resource for the use and benefit of human beings.

The new cosmology blows apart the inherited paradigm.[2] It expands the horizons of possibility beyond the wildest imaginings of human beings. Creation, today sometimes called *multiverse* rather than universe, is viewed as a cosmic enterprise, without beginning or end, evolving toward ever greater complexity, including the paradoxical dynamic of creation-cum-destruction. This is a fundamental paradox, and not a pervasive flaw—an insight that creates substantial challenges for the notion of a divine rescue so basic to the Christian concepts of salvation and redemption.

With the emergence of the new cosmology in the twentieth century, several theological claims had to be reassessed. The notion of God as an external divine creator (manufacturer) began to give way to the notion of co-creation involving each and every

---

[2] How the new cosmology impacts traditional theology, and particularly how we now understand the role of the Holy Spirit in the story of creation, is exquisitely outlined by Leonardo Boff (2015).

constitutive creature, humans and nonhumans alike. Formal religion no longer provided the firm foundation for God's revelation, now regarded as a cosmic unfolding process in which God was fully at work for billions of years before humans or religions ever came to be. Our conventional time spans are now considered heavily anthropocentric, congealing, and destructive. We need to adjust to God's timescales, which are in billions of years and not merely reduced to a few recent millennia.

This same cosmic creation is the seedbed for all forms of aliveness, including that of humans, the most recently derived of all the species (see Oliver 2020). Humans are not in charge of creation and were never intended to be masters. We are servants to an elegant unfolding process. We are invited to be co-creators, enhancing the complexity of creation with the self-reflexive consciousness with which we are uniquely endowed (that is, we think about the fact that we can think). Monotheistic religions, being primarily human-centered, operate out of a very narrow worldview, one rapidly losing credibility in the light of our new understanding of creation today.

As a monotheistic faith system, Christianity faces an acute crisis when confronting the expanded worldview of our time. Scripture scholar N. T. Wright (2013), in his analysis of St. Paul, highlights the fact that creation at large as understood through the Hebrew notion of covenant provides the central focus for our understanding of Jesus as the Christ. Franciscan spiritual writer Richard Rohr (2019) almost single-handedly clarifies the hermeneutical (interpretative) context. While Jesus the historical person is heavily adorned with anthropocentric imperial attributes, Jesus as the Christ represents those universal dimensions of God as the animating and empowering source of all creation.[3]

---

[3] The important distinction here echoes that made by Rudolf Bultmann many years ago: the Jesus of history and the Christ of faith. Rohr seems to me to be more succinct and precise in how he defines the two entities. The *Christ* is an archetypal term with an expansive inclusive

Many of the fertile insights of contemporary cosmology are closely aligned with the worldview embodied in quantum mechanics. So complex and original is the wisdom of quantum physics that mainline science itself has scarcely begun to apprehend and integrate its alternative brand of wisdom. In fact, its foundational tenets are quite simple but earth-shattering in their consequences, as Miriam Therese Winter (2009) and Paul Levy (2018) vividly illustrate.

Foundational to the quantum worldview is the perception that everything in creation is *energy*. It is all that is—and everything that is. Empty space is full of creative energy; the perceived emptiness is actually a fullness. The truth of reality as energy is in the very small—the subatomic realm that is beyond ordinary human comprehension.

In human (scientific) terms we describe energy as a wave-like process, which when humanly observed becomes a particle. Energy waves operate in probabilistic terms. Nothing can be definitively predicted (the uncertainty principle). Energy seems to have a preferred sense of direction—toward greater complexity and creativity. Energy operates according to interdependent principles and does so on a universal scale known as *entanglement*.

Something bigger than cause-and-effect is at work in the quantum realm. There is no neutral observer, but only engaged participants. At the quantum level everything is interrelated, interconnected, and interdependent; reality seems to function optimally when we engage best with this foundational relationality. In the quantum realm, we are dealing with a mystical, experiential perception, a visceral feeling of an energy force that permeates and informs everything in creation. As an energy form, however, it is subtle, pervasive, and infused with an inherent directionality toward meaning and purpose.

---

horizon of meaning, embracing all God's creation; one could describe it as the creativity of God embodied in Jesus. *Jesus* as a name and a title is culturally conditioned, and in the case of Jesus, the conditioning is heavily layered with imperial significance.

Quantum physics is probably the only branch of the human sciences that illuminates this ancient understanding of energy force (more in Schafer 2013). We can also draw on religious and philosophical precedents from the ancient Chinese notion of chi (see Kim 2011; Lee 2014) and from the Vedic concept of *prana* (see McCaul 2007; Maehle 2012). And in part two of this book, I ground the meaning of this energy force in the notion of the Great Spirit. Some scholars, such as British physicist Jude Currivan (2017), feel we have moved beyond quantum physics into the realms of information and consciousness as these engage us through a more holographic understanding of the cosmic creation.

To embrace this new scientific horizon, theology will need to operate on the level of the transpersonal and move beyond the narrow anthropocentric sphere of several previous centuries. The transpersonal is not merely about transcending a narrow human sphere. It also denotes all those other realms of creation that define and influence our humanity, all those other universal and planetary realms without which an authentic human life is not possible. For this undertaking, theology must become multidisciplinary and interdisciplinary, and outgrow the former dualistic split between the sacred and the secular. Integration of diverse empowering resources becomes the new theological horizon.

The Evolutionary Imperative

Beyond the elaborate scientific explanations provided by Charles Darwin and his followers, evolution denotes three foundational processes at work throughout the universe: Growth–Change–Complexity. Everything within and around us grows. We observe the linear life trajectory from original infant forms right through to the maturity of old age. More common, however, is the cyclic process, observable in seasonal patterns and changes. The birthing and dying are readily observed, but contrary to the linear view, here we see revitalized breakthroughs after each dying.

This brings us to the second major feature of the evolutionary process: change. Nothing in creation is static and stable. Everything changes, and in fact changes all the time. Without such change no organic life-form holds any enduring meaning. Every cell in the human body dies and is replaced every seven years. Without such consistent change, life as we know it simply would not exist.

Inherent to such change is the notion of decline, decay, and death. In many of nature's processes, the death of the old seems to be a prerequisite for the birth of the new. The tree must shed its leaves in autumn and winter before the fresh foliage of the springtime can emerge. For humans, death is a highly problematic phenomenon, a curse that hopefully some day we will conquer and eliminate. Alas, it is a bizarre hope that seems to have no sense of how central and necessary death is for the ongoing life of all planetary beings.

Of all the world religions, Christianity holds a highly distorted view of death and dying (closely followed by Islam), almost entirely stripped of any evolutionary perspective. According to Paul's letter to the Romans, death had "reigned" over all the children of Adam (cf. Rom 5:14) and "the wages of sin is death" (cf. Rom 6:21–23). "For when we were in the realm of the flesh, the sinful passions aroused by the law were at work in us, so that we bore fruit for death" (Rom 7:5). For Paul, death is caused by Adam's fall from grace, and thereafter is a curse that all humans must endure. Although the death (and resurrection) of Jesus rescues humans from the sting of death, it still remains an enigma that it seems can only be resolved in a life hereafter.

From an evolutionary perspective, two issues need to be addressed and reconstituted: (1) Humans have never lived in a sinless, idyllic realm free from corruption and death—death has always been an integral part of our evolutionary becoming; (2) Death is an integral dimension of all organic life—it is not an evil to be tolerated or eliminated. If some day humans get rid of death, then life as we know it will come to naught.

Consequently, the Christian notion of Jesus coming to rescue us from death and abolish death forever is an evolutionary contradiction that is likely to contribute to meaningless death in our world rather than lead to hope and new freedom. The Christian notion of redemption wrought by the death of Jesus on the cross is increasingly regarded as meaningless theology. The notion wins support mainly from the millions of people around our world condemned to poverty and powerlessness; the redemptive myth is indeed an opium that comforts and consoles but does little to liberate people from their crippling destitution.

Our evolutionary understanding of life radically changes the very foundations of our faith, particularly the Christian focus on the death and resurrection of Jesus, with the ensuing doctrines of salvation and redemption. What theology has long regarded as the sinful plight of a deviant humanity, evolution perceives as the enduring incompleteness required by an open-ended, unfolding creation in which nothing is whole or perfect, yet everything is open to empowering transformation; the movement from the older to the more integrated, evolutionary approach is traced by Jesuit theologian Roger Haight (2019). In Christian terms, the focus shifts from the once-and-for-all divine rescue made possible by the death and resurrection of the historical Jesus, to the empowering dynamism of God's creativity throughout creation, and the incarnational potentiality of the reign of God, activated anew in the life and death of the historical Jesus.

Theology, Old and New

This opening chapter poses the question: *What is theology?* Paul Tillich's definition still holds: it engages the search for what is of ultimate concern to the human spirit.[4] Historically, we understood the Bible to be the resource that would connect us with, and ground us in, the true authentic revelation that God has made

---

[4] More on Tillich's empowering theology in Pryor and Stahl (2018).

once and forever. In this understanding, the fundamental truths engaging the theologian are already given in sacred Scripture; the theologian's task is to explain and illuminate their meaning for different cultural contexts. And in that undertaking, Jesus, as the imperial Christ, holds a central place. Jesus is the only authentic revelation of the one ruling God.

One attempt to dislodge the imperial metaphysical deity was that of process theology, a development of the twentieth century with American philosopher Alfred North Whitehead (1861–1947) as its primary inspiration.[5] In fact, Whitehead sought to transcend not one but three inherited images of God: (1) God as an imperial ruler, favored particularly by Roman culture; (2) God as a personification of moral energy, the ruthless moralist, upheld by the Hebrew prophets; and (3) God as the ultimate philosophical principle, Aristotle's unmoved mover. Of the three, it is the third—Aristotle's influence—that still continues to influence our understanding of God, and theology generally, particularly under the rubric of Scholasticism.

Process thought challenges the inherited metaphysical attributes of God as an all-knowing and all-powerful force who never changes and operates beyond the influence of a vacillating, evolv-

---

[5] *Process and Reality: An Essay in Cosmology* (1929) is the most frequently referenced work of Whitehead in relation to process philosophy and theology. The main application of Whitehead's position was developed by his pupil, American philosopher Charles Hartshorne (1897–2000), whose main works include *The Divine Relativity: A Social Conception of God* (New Haven, CT: Yale University Press, 1948) and *The Logic of Perfection: And Other Essays in Neoclassical Metaphysics* (LaSalle, IL: Open Court Publishing, 1962). Contemporary exponents referenced in the present work include John D. Caputo (2013), Catherine Keller (2003), and Roland Faber (2017). The views of Whitehead and Hartshorne should also be distinguished from those that affirm that the divine being, by an act of self-limitation, opens itself to influence from the world. Some neo-Thomists hold this view, and a group of Evangelical Christian philosophers, calling themselves "open theists," promote similar ideas.

ing universe. Instead, process theologians claim that God operates by persuasion rather than by coercion, respecting the freedom and creativity of universal life and itself affected by the ever changing dynamics of creation at large. This does not mean that God is simply a predetermined outcome of an evolving world that one day can dispense with God entirely. Rather what is envisaged is a transpersonal, archetypal life force through which creation is forever coming into being and co-evolving with all the other creatures that inhabit such a universe.

On the problem of evil, process theologians distinguish between natural evil and moral evil (sin). For process thinkers, destruction, pain, and suffering are inherent to creation's evolutionary course, and without this imperfect world no freedom nor creativity would exist. God participates in—suffers with—the evolving creation. Much of the moral evil in the world arises from our human desire to modify and control the inherent suffering of creation at large—described in chapter 5 of this book as the great paradox. In adopting this approach, process theology is not addressing a God who becomes so weak that many would consider such a God not worth believing in; rather it throws the onus onto us, humans, to take a more direct responsibility for our contribution to the meaningless suffering in the world, and challenges us to work collaboratively with God for the reduction and elimination of such suffering.

Process theology was one of several movements in the twentieth century to loosen the Greek metaphysical grip on our understanding of God, to move away from the imperial divine tyrant to a more incarnational immersion of the Holy One, not merely in our human midst but in the midst of creation at large. Roland Faber (2017) describes the shift in terms of three major contours: (1) an expanded relationship between society, philosophy, and mysticism; (2) a reformulation of philosophy between poetry and mathematics; and (3) a new integration between philosophical cosmology and religion in an evolutionary and multireligious context.

In a word, theology embraces a new horizon: one that is multicultural, multireligious, and multidisciplinary, transcending inherited metaphysical categories and outgrowing the dualistic split between sacred and secular. This expansive landscape is outlined in part two of the present work. My approach differs from that of process theology insofar as I strive not to speculate about the nature of God. (That realm belongs to the theologian rather than to a social scientist.) If creation is God's primary revelation for us—the domain where the divine creativity has been at work for several millennia—then why not seek out deeper spiritual meaning through the creation of which we are an integral part, rather than using inflated human rationality to engage with lofty religious heights far beyond our powers of comprehension?[6] Creation is the context for all life processes, including, I suspect, the deepest insights we can ever hope to achieve into the nature of God.

Today, the theological landscape has changed enormously. Metaphysical attributes, adopted at one time to understand and explain (prove) the existence of God, no longer carry weight nor credibility. We need to incorporate transhistorical, archetypal understandings, as in Richard Rohr's (2019) distinction between Jesus and the Christ. Furthermore, there is the mystical perspective, advocating that the less said about God, the better! Instead let's focus on the mystery that is creation itself, God's primary revelation of God's self, and as we grasp the deeper meaning of creation, we can begin to discern more deeply the reality we call God.

---

[6] As stated by evolutionary theologian Ilia Delio (2008, 62), "The world is created as a means of God's self-revelation so that, like a mirror or footprint, it might lead us to love and praise the Creator. We are created to read the book of creation so that we may know the Author of Life. This book of creation is an expression of who God is and is meant to lead humans to what it signifies, namely, the eternal Trinity of dynamic, self-diffusive love."

A Spirit-Evolving God

Today, the God question is open to multiple meanings, and the more open we can keep them, the better our chances of transcending the idolatry of the past that often reduced God (and Jesus) to an inflated human projection. Personally, I find the notion of the Great Spirit a valuable starting point in our human attempts to discern the meaning of God. The Great Spirit is the name adopted by indigenous peoples (all over the world) for divine reality. It is not so much a transcendent, personal being, as conventionally understood, but a transpersonal energy force imbuing all creation with empowering creativity (more in O'Murchu 2011).

Access to the Great Spirit is obtained through the land—and this is not to be confused with either pantheism or panentheism. As earthlings, born out of the living earth and forever dependent upon it for survival and flourishing, we come to know the Great Spirit through our convivial relationship with creation at large. In this context, our indigenous peoples do not worship the Great Spirit. They forever strive to work collaboratively with the Spirit; such collaboration is mediated mainly through rites and rituals, many of which are focused on the fertility of soil and land.

When we engage the notion of the Great Spirit as the entry point for accessing the divine imperative, then several of our inherited religious beliefs are no longer sustainable. If we put the Spirit first, the original energetic source of creativity evidenced in the opening verse of the book of Genesis, then we need to reframe and reconfigure our understanding of God as Trinity. The Father/Creator can only create in the power of the energizing Spirit. As I later elaborate, such a creative force is better understood through the metaphor of the Great Birther rather than the Great Ruler. Then we can rescue Jesus from the anthropocentric Son of the ruling Father, and reenvision his role within the African notion of the Ancestors, Jesus being an archetypal figure reconnecting humans with our great ancestral African story, going back some 7 million years (more in O'Murchu 2008).

Today, all of our theological horizons are expanded and enlarged. The earlier landmarks—the Judeo-Christian Scripture, Jesus as Messiah, revelation of divine truth, inspiration of Scripture, the church, ecclesiastical teaching authority, sacraments, salvation, and so on—still hold religious significance but need to be radically reframed in terms of our postmodern evolutionary culture. Even the language with which we name these landmarks has become archaic and irrelevant.

Before moving on to the evolutionary vision, which will be the major part of this book (in part two), I wish to note briefly two elements foundational to our inherited understanding of theology still extensively used in Christian circles today, namely *tradition* and the *focus on our flawed human condition*. In popular parlance, tradition denotes that which we cling to, foundational truths that have never changed and never can. Theologically, tradition is rooted in Scripture (with a tendency to interpret it literally) and passed on to subsequent generations by the teaching authority of the church.

Contemporary theologians and Scripture scholars frequently allude to *reworking the tradition*. Often the problem is that they don't go deep enough to recapture foundational truth. Similarly, science once championed a process known as *recapitulation*, the biogenetic law historically associated with Ernst Haeckel (1834–1919). Haeckel posited that species at the embryonic stage appear to go through developmental stages that mirror their evolutionary history. Although the specifics of his law have been rejected by modern scientists, the general concept may yet be useful for understanding evolutionary development—like an athlete preparing to execute a long jump in track and field, we step back several stages from the jumping-off point in order to gather momentum to leap forward several steps. Metaphorically, we are drawing energy from the deep past in order to engage more creatively with the emerging future.

From an evolutionary perspective, we need to honor the inherited wisdom, recognizing how it served us well within past cultural contexts, congruent perhaps with the prevailing consciousness of the time. But evolution never allows us to rest with any one prevailing view. It urges (lures) us forward to ever new and promising horizons. In gratitude we receive from the past, but in hopeful anticipation we open our hearts and minds to the creative Spirit, the enduring lure of the future. In that spirit of openness we review past theological paradigms, not merely to criticize what became congealed in the ideologies of power and patriarchy, but what the Spirit bestowed that endures across time, and now informs the evolutionary horizons that call us to new modes of theological engagement.

Second, we need to redress the flawed human condition at the heart of our inherited theological wisdom, an issue that also preoccupies several other major religious systems. This is one pertinent example of our human tendency to read reality superficially and not in depth. Ever since the Agricultural Revolution some ten thousand years ago, we have been enmeshed in a deviant anthropology largely because our relationship with the surrounding creation became highly dysfunctional. For a range of complex reasons—partially clarified in chapter 7 of this volume—we lost our grounding as a species living convivially with the living earth itself. We set out to manipulate and control the entire creation to our own primary advantage. In that process we lost our deep organic interconnectedness with the web of life.

Because of the narrow time frame within which all religions operate—a mere few thousand years—we end up with religious dogmas almost totally devoid of historical and cultural perspective. Today, our theology needs to be reframed within a universe at least 13.7 billion years old, an organic life process of some 4 billion years, and a human evolutionary story of 7 *million years*. We have come to realize that our human story was very different from the long-assumed primitive barbarity. To the contrary, I argue, we seem to have gotten it right more often than not in terms of achieving a harmonious existence—because we remained very close to the dynamic flow of the natural world. As we become ever more acquainted with that long, sacred story, the claim that we are a fundamentally flawed species (original sin) becomes ever more incredulous and theologically unsustainable (more in O'Murchu 2018).

Nothing utopian in this claim! Two major issues obstruct our view of this more wholesome possibility regarding humanity's relationship to the natural world. First, the time factor, conditioned as we are by a suffocating reductionistic view situating the human within the context of a mere few thousand years, when in fact our true human story is one of 7 million years (more in chapter 9). And second, the cerebral patriarchal arrogance, with its pinnacle in classical Greek philosophy, claiming that only the human species (in fact, only the male members) is endowed with a soul, and therefore has the right to rule over everything else in creation.

We need to move beyond the notion of original sin, the theological view that we are foundationally a flawed species because of our ancient rebellion against God in the heavenly realm. Instead, I suggest the major flaw we need to deal with today is the double deviation highlighted above: (a) a time constriction that is stifling us to death and (b) overreliance on rational imperialism. No God or Savior can rescue us from that plight. We ourselves have invented the ensuing alienation; it is up to us to resolve it.

2

The Codependent Paradigm

*So deep is this distortion that I have become convinced
that we must put an end to atonement theology or there
will be no future for the Christian faith.*

John Shelby Spong

*The presence of the wide evolving cosmos calls for a
genuinely new paradigm, different from the anthropo
centric concern with human sin in the context of feudal
obligations. We need to turn the page on the satisfaction
theory and allow it to take a well-deserved rest.*

Elizabeth Johnson

Throughout much of the modern world, the Christian churches
are largely preoccupied with the plight of a deviant human species that needs to be rescued and redeemed. And Jesus is the one
and only Savior through which this can be accomplished. An old
theological paradigm still prevails with a stubborn resistant dura-
bility. It is usually depicted as a threefold process consisting of
Creation–Fall–Redemption.

Although creation in this approach is often described as "the
work of God's hands," both the outcome and God, the creative

life force, end up in a highly problematic quagmire. The creator is postulated as the all-powerful, ruling deity, reigning from above the sky, before whom nothing existed, who creates totally from the beginning and exclusively by his own divine power—hence the notion of *creatio ex nihilo* (creation out of nothing).

Despite the grandeur and splendor frequently attributed to the divine Creator, this male divine figurehead delivers a creation that is quite problematic. It is deemed to be permanently flawed, allegedly because of an angelic rebellion in heaven in some distant past time. And this built-in flaw is such that it can only be rectified by divine intervention. Strangely, the Creator himself, despite all his magnificent divine power, seems unable to rectify the sinful mess, and so has to resort to another outcome: the sacrifice of his beloved Son, a strategy that, in the Middle Ages, came to be known as the atonement theory.

From earliest times, Christian scholars proposed an alternative theory of the *felix culpa* (happy fault) whereby God might have willed things this way to bring about a greater good. St. Ambrose speaks of the fortunate ruin of Adam in the Garden of Eden in that his sin brought more good to humanity than if the human had retained an original foundational innocence. The Latin expression *felix culpa* derives from St. Augustine's claim that "God judged it better to bring good out of evil than not to permit any evil to exist."[1] Centuries later, Thomas Aquinas cited this line when he explained how the principle that "God allows evil to happen in order to bring a greater good therefrom"[2] underlies the causal relation between original sin and the divine Redeemer's incarnation, thus concluding that a higher state is not inhibited by sin. This line of argument holds little water today for a growing body of more reflectively critical Christians.

According to this paradigm, the third part of the construct—redemption—belongs exclusively to Christianity. Only the Chris-

---

[1] Augustine, *Enchiridion* VIII.27.
[2] Thomas Aquinas, *Summa Theologiae* 3, q.1, a.3, ad 3.

tian Jesus can make salvation possible for all humankind. Jesus was God's conscious choice to undo the sin of Adam. Only Jesus could do it, and according to this paradigm, only Jesus created the possibility of a breakthrough from the trap of sin and enslavement. None of the other religions are capable of delivering this redemptive outcome. Only Christianity has the monopoly on grace and salvation.

It is unclear what exactly Jesus achieved by giving his life on the cross for sinners and for the salvation of the world. Humans are still prone to sin and temptation, and Christians over the centuries have failed rather dismally to be a redemptive force either for humanity or for the wider creation. To the contrary, Christians have created and supported violence, warfare, oppression, and a frequently reckless disregard for the earth and its resources. And the Christian churches themselves have colluded with patriarchal domination, misogyny, racism, slavery, and colonial oppression.

The Anthropocentric Deviation

The root of the problem of evil might well have to do with the anthropocentric overlay. Humans seem to be the cause of the entire cosmic disarray, in view of the fact that creation had flourished for billions of years before humans ever evolved. Allegedly, everything became corrupted because of a human rebellion in the heavenly realm, creating a preposterous myth that goes like this:

> Everything in heaven was whole and harmonious till one powerful angel, called Lucifer, got strange ideas, feeling that he could both challenge and transcend the mighty power of God himself. And he persuaded other angels that this feat could be accomplished. They say pride was Lucifer's downfall, leading to the great sin of disobedience. Michael, another powerful archangel, got whiff of what was brewing and rallied an alternative force. Battle broke out between the two groups. Michael and his

cohort proved to be victorious, kicking Lucifer (hence Satan or the Dragon) out of Heaven. The defeated angels landed on earth, condemned thereafter to a non-angelic status, called human nature. They began propagating through sexual intercourse, thus spreading their evil contagion not merely across the emerging human population but right into every aspect of creation. And the conduit through which the contagion spread was sex, understood to be a fierce instinctual drive.[3]

For much of Christian history, this myth was deemed to be literally true. Today, it is still cherished by fundamentalist scholars who surface a range of texts (mainly from the books of Daniel in the Old Testament and from Revelation in the New Testament) to substantiate the myth. More progressive scholars do not take it literally; in fact, many dismiss the theory of original sin as having no basis in the Christian Scriptures (see Spong 1998; Williams 2001; Wiley 2002; McFarland 2010).[4]

The problem is anthropological and not merely theological. Humans are deemed to be the most superior creatures in all of creation, and if humans don't get it right, then—according to this ideology—nothing will be right anywhere in the universe. There follow a number of deviant elements needing more discerning attention in our time.

First of all, the notion of an original utopian state in which all humans coexisted in harmonic innocence makes no sense in an evolutionary universe. It is a deluded belief, based on the notion of an omnipotent, perfect God as postulated by monotheism and Greek metaphysics, which, in turn, postulates an original perfect human alongside the all-powerful Deity.

---

[3] Diarmuid O'Murchu, *Beyond Original Sin* (Maryknoll, NY: Orbis Books, 2018), 26.

[4] For an up-to-date overview of the theological thinking on original sin, particularly within an evolutionary optic, see the informed and comprehensive treatment by Haight (2019, 113–41).

Second, Lucifer's hunger for power marks a primordial irruption of the human urge for absolute control. This urge is not born from some ancient Satanic instinct but from humanity's own confused patriarchal projections. In other words, we seek out mythological, angelic figureheads to compensate for our inability to obtain the quality—and quantity—of the earthly power that we desire.

Third, how do humans try to obtain that power? By setting up a demonized, dualistic force with which we can engage in battle. The heavenly battle, therefore, is a mirror image of the earthly strategy of competitive conflict adopted by patriarchal males in order to reclaim their power. This perverse hunger for power all too quickly becomes addictive and compulsive to a point where even God himself becomes a violent oppressor.

Fourth, pride and disobedience become the primary sins that preoccupy the patriarchs. They continue to be major moral infringements for all religions today that still cling to the codependent paradigm.

Fifth, humans assume an inflated existence, what Steve Taylor (2005) calls the *ego explosion*. They become the superior species, seeking to control everything within and around them. Creation becomes a mere commodity for human usufruct, the mechanistic view of creation, so problematic even for mainline science in our time.

Sixth, in terms of the growth and flourishing of the human, the dichotomy between power and powerlessness controls and pollutes the entire plot. Most people will end up trapped in powerlessness and can therefore never hope to realize the fuller potential of their God-given humanity.

This leads us, finally, to the reason why I name this a *codependent* paradigm. In its broadest definition, *codependency* refers to people who cannot function from the basis of a healthy self-image because their thinking and behavior are organized around another person, process, or substance. In the present context I use the term to define a prolonged sense of childlike dependence in a culture that inhibits or prevents people from becoming more authentically adult. Traditionally, Christianity (and other religions too) has inculcated such deep levels of guilt and unworthiness that many people lived in irrational fear of others (and of God), sometimes for an entire lifetime.

The Flawed Creation

This codependent paradigm is concerned almost exclusively with humans and their sinful, fallen state. This view of reality, whereby we set humans above and beyond everything else in creation, tends to be described as *anthropocentric*. Simply put, only humans matter. Creation is viewed as the cultural context in which humans happen to be situated, and it is not a happy place to be. No meaningful explanation is offered on why humans occupy this cultural niche. One wonders if this paradigm really accepts the fact that God is the creator of the universe.

One thing is very clear in this outline: humans are not meant to feel at home in creation. They inhabit a vale of tears; their days are spent in anguish and suffering. The best they can do—with the grace of God—is to tolerate their unfortunate situation and trust that God in the end will enable them to escape to the happiness of eternal life in another world, outside and beyond this corrupted creation.

The only hope for humans is to belong to the church and obey all its laws and rules in such a way that they will obtain the reward of eternal life after death. Only the church, established and sustained by Godly males, has the monopoly of salvation. Only the church can get us from this sinful world to the other world of eternal happiness. But the church can only assist us if we submit totally to its requirements for right living.

Of course, such a church wants us to treat creation with respect, but mainly by keeping humans aloof as far as possible from intimate engagement with creation's processes. A more convivial relationship with the earth and its organic processes is envisaged largely in terms of struggle and pain; humans have to endure the painful length of their days until the final liberation arrives.

Here I briefly outline the first element of the triune package: Creation–Fall–Redemption. First, for a growing body of contemporary Christians, the God who creates this strangely deranged world is rapidly losing faith allegiance, in the face of which theology needs to engage a substantial task of deconstruction. Our inherited created story smacks of large-scale patriarchal manipulation, in which the all-powerful creator himself becomes enmeshed in self-destructive power games out of which no living entity—humans included—can grow or flourish.

Second, the proposed Christian solution—faith in and through the church—is becoming equally unsustainable for a growing number of adult believers. All Christian denominations are currently experiencing significant numerical decline, Pentecostalism being a notable exception.[5] Increasingly the Christian churches are perceived to be authoritarian hierarchical structures, ultimately concerned with their own survival and perpetuation, and unable to deliver the gospel empowerment necessary to engage life authentically amid the complexities of our time.

The Fall and Redemption

Consequently, two features loom large in the contemporary understanding of the church: the two remaining elements of the triune structure, namely fall and redemption. When these items come to the fore, then the notion of church as an empowering

---

[5] The Pentecostal movement is often criticized for the codependency it creates among gullible and often vulnerable people, with highly questionable allurements like that of the prosperity gospel. One of the better-known Pentecostal theologians, Amos Yong, attributes the success of the movement thus: "Rather, it is the Pentecostal form of worship and spirituality that is embodied and affective, rather than primarily cerebral, that not only distinguishes Pentecostalism from other Christian traditions but also accounts for its expansion across the majority world" (in Tan and Tran 2016, 51).

community—think of the Pauline ecclesial groups—is compromised. Even more seriously, the theological notion of church as servant and herald of the new reign of God (the kingdom) is no longer honored as our primary concern ("Seek *first* the kingdom"—Mt 6:33). These are the subverted elements that need to be retrieved and reconstructed, as I indicate in part two. First, however, we need to understand why the fall-redemption construct gained such prominence and how we might now deconstruct it in contemporary theology.

In terms of the New Testament, St. Paul provides the earliest thinking on the notion of redemption, which for Paul is intimately connected with the fall of humankind, as symbolically represented by the first Adam. For Paul, fall and redemption go together. Most Pauline commentators devote significant space and attention to the notion of redemption, assuming that the fall is an issue already given, and that it therefore needs little explanation.

In fact, it is not entirely clear when, where, and how the notion of a fallen humanity originated. The previously postulated harmonious condition of human beings suggests that creation itself was also whole and integral, without flaw, and without any alteration to its pure, unchanging nature. In this case, the idyllic creation is an indestructible entity, perhaps a mirror reflection of the absolute integrity of the Godhead itself, but existing on its own apart from God, its creator and sustainer; thus, one assumes that the cosmic-earthly realm somehow resembles the heavenly sphere. Or is there any need to postulate a heavenly state until after the fall of humans? Only then does the perfect heaven make sense as the dualistic opposite of the corrupted earth.

All we can be sure about (it seems) is the plight of the earthly creation *after the fall of the human*—and, presumably, the entire cosmic creation as well. In the tradition there is nothing to suggest that fallen humans caused the cosmic-earthly creation to become corrupted. Rather the corrupt state of the natural world emerges simultaneously with the rebellion of the human against God. From that point on, the struggle and alienation of the human-as-human seems intertwined with a deviant creation, which in its alienation from God can distract humans from the things of God and plunge them deeper into temptation and sin.

As with the human, so also with the earth. The plight of sin and corruption can only be upended by a special divine intervention. Moreover, it seems that the rescue (redemption) of the human is a precondition for restoring creation itself to a state of wholeness and integrity. St. Paul, in his allusion to creation groaning in Romans 8:22–24, seems to be suggesting that it is only after the "revealing of the children of God that creation will be set free from bondage to decay and obtain the freedom of the glory of the children of God." For Paul, the liberation of creation seems to depend on humans finding their freedom—in and through the death and resurrection of Jesus the messianic Christ.

In Paul's vision, salvation/redemption is an extremely complex reality (see Wright 2013; Ware 2019). It continues to be a contentious subject among biblical scholars with no single uniform understanding. The following are some of the key elements relevant for past understandings, and for future interpretative possibilities.

First, in dealing with the death and resurrection of Jesus, Paul is more concerned with laying out the cosmic significance of the death of Jesus as the Christ rather than with its historical circumstances, and he communicates this significance above all in terms of its benefits for humankind. In subsequent theological reflection, these benefits have been developed under the various theories of atonement. After centuries of debate it is now difficult to read Paul without the overlay of one or more of the so-called classical theories of the atonement: the *dramatic theory*, which portrays the saving work of Christ as a cosmic drama of conflict and victory; the *satisfaction theory*, with its often-held corollary, penal or forensic satisfaction, with Jesus considered to be the one who renders satisfaction to God; and the *moral influence* theory, which concentrates on the cross as a demonstration to humanity of God's boundless love that is to be emulated.

Second, within this cosmic context, Paul is dealing primary with the Jesus who represents the messianic Christ, and not to what happened in and through the historical Jesus.[6] Today, Pauline scholarship emphasizes the central importance of the Jewishness of Paul, which leaves us with quite a dilemma: to the Jewish people, the notion of a crucified Messiah would be scandalous and abhorrent. Is Paul, therefore, transcending the conventional understanding of Judaism in his desire to embrace the Gentiles? For Paul, therefore, does the cross signify not so much the death of the historical Jesus but rather the paradoxical triumph of the messianic Christ, as illustrated in 1 Corinthians 15:3–17: "Christ died for us in accordance with the scriptures; that he was buried; that he was raised on the third day in accordance with the scriptures. . . . If Christ has not been raised, then empty is our preaching; empty, too, your faith. . . . Your faith is in vain; you are still in your sins"?

Third, Paul's understanding of sin and righteousness must also be heard within a cosmic context. For Paul, sin is a cumulative force of evil exercising power over humanity. In Paul's time, the universe is perceived as full of hostile forces over which humans "subject to the Law" (of Judaism) have little or no control. As indicated in Romans 6:6–11, the death of Jesus is the price paid to release humans from the grip of the "law," this state of

---

[6] Earlier in this book, I referenced Richard Rohr (2019) for his thorough and original analysis of the distinction between Jesus and the Christ. According to Rohr, "Paul uses the single word 'Jesus' without adding 'Christ' or 'Lord' only five times in all his authentic letters" (2019, 196). It is often noted that Paul never alludes to the central features describing Jesus in the Gospels, such as the role of the kingdom of God, the Sermon on the Mount, the parables, or the miracles. In fact, when Paul refers to the gospel, his sole concern is the death and resurrection of the messianic Jesus, as the Christ, which needs to be understood in archetypal terms (with global implications) and not in its frequently understood imperial meaning. However, Paul's stance on imperial posturing is also quite complex, as indicated in the compendium edited by Christopher D. Stanley (2011).

sin-unto-death. For Paul, Jesus in his life and death is the representative human, representative of fallen humanity; by living out that fallenness and overcoming it in the power of the resurrection, he becomes representative of new life, of the new human.

Contemporary Pauline scholars such as N. T. Wright claim that Paul's starting point is creation at large rather than the human being. A consistently Jewish thinker, Paul never imagines that creation is evil; it is the good creation of the good God, and to be enjoyed as such. But, in line with much apocalyptic thought, Paul believes that God is planning to renew creation, to bring it out of its present state of decay and death and into the new world where it would find its true fulfillment (cf. Rom 8:18–27). Paul does not mention the cross in that specific passage, but rather the sufferings of Christians, which are, for him, the sharing of Christ's sufferings, and these hold the key to the current state of affairs through which the world must pass to attain its final deliverance from decay.

Despite the plea of a scholar like N. T. Wright that we view Paul's vision in terms of the renewed covenantal creation, it is difficult to transcend the very overt anthropocentric focus of Paul's theology and the ensuing soteriology. It is the plight and pain of the human condition that preoccupy Paul. It is also the central focus of his understanding of the death and resurrection of Jesus, the unique divine deliverance whereby the old Adam can become a new creation in Christ. And if the human world can be rescued from its sinful plight, then there is a chance that everything else in creation can be set aright.

From Paul Back to Jesus

The Gospels' approach to the death and resurrection of Jesus is very different from that of Paul. While the focus is still on the human sinful condition, the resolution of that debilitating state takes a very different turn. Cynthia Bourgeault (2008, 21) makes the interesting observation that Western Christianity has been preoccupied with salvation and soteriology—to make up for the flaw left because of the sin of Adam—whereas Eastern Christianity is much more concerned about the wisdom necessary for good living, which she describes as *sophiology*. The former emphasizes what Jesus did for us because essentially we are disempowered, helpless creatures, while the latter underlines mutual empowerment—a quality of engagement with life that the historical Jesus embraced as a process of human transformation—and implies that, inspired by the primordial example of Jesus, we can also realize it in our own lives (cf. Patterson 2004).

In the original Aramaic of Jesus's time, there was no word for *salvation*. In the Aramaic New Testament, two words are used: one of these is *chai*, meaning "life" or "to vivify," and the other is *p'rak*, which comes from a root meaning "to separate" and invokes the image of one being "rescued" by being separated from a threat. This latter meaning clearly echoes the atoning nature of Jesus's death and resurrection, portraying Jesus, as Paul does, in the traditional role of the great rescuer.

Of particular interest for the present work is the way in which patriarchal kingly power is woven into the passion narrative of the Gospels and holds the reader in its grip. It feels like a story of high drama, and is sometimes depicted as such, when in truth the act of crucifixion was a savage, brutal affair that no responsible person would want to honor, acclaim, or even record. The trials of Jesus make the plot more colorful and alluring—six in all, culminating in Pilate's death sentence for a crime of trying to usurp kingly power (the allegation that Jesus claimed to be king of the Jews). The trials, as described, infringe on several principles of Roman jurisprudence, and have long been regarded as fictitious or as mock trials at best. So why was it so important for the Gospel writers to include and emphasize such trials?

Are we witnessing an enduring fixation with divine kingship, with Jesus as a perceived messianic prophet, who had to be of kingly origin, and therefore would have had to have a fair and just trial? A king could not have been killed without some attempt at juridical justice. So the Gospel writers invent a legal travesty with Jesus consistently depicted as the mythic hero, adorned with kingly might, as in John 18:37. And after the death of the royal One, the Gospel writers have to make sure that there is something akin to a royal burial. The notion that Jesus's body might have been dumped in a pit for wild animals to consume—which is typically what happened to crucified subversives—is a prospect that must not even be entertained when dealing with somebody of noble, royal status.

Power, and not sanctity (divinity), is what dictates much of the passion narrative. And the entire story must be made to look and feel heroic. Ideally, as in John's Gospel, the condemned hero must be seen not merely to survive but to triumph. All too easily, then, the death becomes an end in itself, the ultimate paradoxical triumph of the hero. Emulation of the death will later be perceived to be necessary for those who are called to discipleship. Correspondingly, the archetypal empowerment of the life of Jesus fades into the background, and for much of the Christian era, his life was viewed mainly as preparation for the grand finale that alone could deliver divine salvation.

In an oft-cited text, Crossan (1996) interprets the passion narrative as *prophesy historicized* rather than history remembered. Key texts and insights from the Hebrew Scriptures—especially from Psalms, Isaiah, the Prophets, and the Wisdom literature—were employed, first, to make sense of the violent and untimely death of Jesus, and second, to augment belief in the messianic status attributed to Jesus by the early followers. The end result is a vastly embellished proclamation, much like a historical tribute to a fallen hero. The downfall of the hero became the alluring myth, while the heroic transformation of Jesus's earthly life and ministry was diverted and subverted.

Despite the elaborate details in all four Gospels, we know virtually nothing about the passion and death of Jesus. We have a narrative based on the faith convictions of the early followers who attempted to make sense out of Jesus's untimely death by extrapolating from the Hebrew Scriptures events and sayings that seemed to be pointing to Jesus and helped make sense out of his death, and that were woven into a melodramatic story that became the passion-cum-resurrection narratives in Gospel lore.

If we want something akin to a historical backdrop, we are—as Crossan (1996, 17–18) suggests—on more solid ground when we invoke the first Roman War of 66–70 CE, in which the Temple in Jerusalem was destroyed and thousands of innocent people were killed. Much of the calamity, injustice, and violence associated with the death of Jesus—and vividly portrayed in Mel Gibson's film *The Passion of the Christ*—was probably inspired by that historical event, as was a great deal of the apocalyptic material in Mark 13 and elsewhere in the Gospels.

The truth behind the melodramatic detail is not difficult to discern. Crucifixion was a form of death reserved, not even for hardened criminals, but for subversives, for those perceived to be a threat to the prevailing power. Jesus was a subversive, mainly because of how he activated empowerment among the masses. Although some scholars argue that Jesus may have been an anti-Roman protagonist (Brandon 1967; Bermejo-Rubio 2014), inciting violent rebellion against the empire, most view Jesus as a nonviolent revolutionary, but promoting forms of empowerment—particularly among the disenfranchised—that quite quickly (it seems) came to be seen as a serious threat to imperial law and order.

The authorities seized him at an opportune moment—with or without the collusion of some of his close followers (e.g., Judas)—and proceeded to subject him to a quick, brutal death, without dignity or mercy. *There is nothing salvific or redemptive in the death of Jesus*. It was the ultimate price he paid for his radical, subversive, empowering mission, the prospect facing every prophetic visionary. In the case of Jesus, the locus for empowerment is in his *life*, not in his death.

"One of the great mistakes of Christian theology," writes Scripture scholar Stephen J. Patterson, has been our attempt to understand the death and resurrection of Jesus apart from his life. His death and resurrection are directly related to his life; they issue from it. . . . To the followers and friends of Jesus, his death was important in its particularity—as the fate of him who said and did certain things, who stood for something so important to him that he was willing to give his life for it. That something was the vision of life he called the empire of God. If this vision was indeed God's empire, then the bearer of this vision was not dead. No executioner could kill what he was. To kill Jesus, you would have to kill the vision. That is what the cross could not do. (2004, 2, 127)

And it is in his life that Jesus suffers most intensely, enduring the taunts and ridicule of opponents, the misunderstandings of those whom he tried to help, and perhaps most bewildering of all, the dumbness and disappointment of those on whom he relied (e.g., "Do you still not perceive or understand?" [Mk 8:17]). Yes, Jesus suffered, and so will those who are committed to the new reign of God created in Jesus's name. But that suffering is in life, and for life, and not some pseudo-mystical ideology that sanctions death and construes violent death as being somehow synonymous with salvation and holiness.

Beyond the Disempowering Cross

It seems to me that there is a distinctive difference between the suffering of Jesus at the service of new life (epitomized in the empowering vision of the kingdom of God) and the understandings of Christian suffering that emerged over time. For instance, in the Catacombs in Rome, we find no images of a crucified Christ, nor of a God in judgment demanding that people suffer to make up for sin or wrongdoing. To the contrary, we find images celebrating the luscious life of nature, depicting the paradise in which every creature feels at home. Brock and Parker (2008, ix–x,

60–63) claim that the martyrs associated with the Catacombs embraced martyrdom not to win eternal salvation in a life hereafter, but that through their sufferings they would help to bring about paradise on this earth. In other words, they did not suffer for the sake of being redeemed through suffering; rather they envisaged their sufferings—and their deaths—as serving a release of new life for other persons, creatures, and for creation at large.

Redemption through suffering is a historically fraught notion and more complex than most people realize. Salvation through the power of the cross is assumed to be a Christian conviction that prevailed from earliest times, and already in the writings of St. Paul we find evidence for this outlook. Most church historical texts highlight martyrdom among early Christians and hail the martyrs as outstanding Christians whose holiness was exemplary precisely because they suffered so much. Suffering comes to be understood as the perennial Christian virtue, a more reliable guarantee to obtain our heavenly reward in a life hereafter. From this time on, suffering for the sake of suffering becomes central to the notion of Christian salvation and redemption, with the historical Jesus upheld as the paradigmatic victim, whose violent death and suffering arrested the power of sin and opened the gates of heaven for sinful creatures. And those who suffered most were the ones who stood the best chance of inheriting eternal life in heaven.

Why did Christians become so enamored with redemptive violence, and more importantly how do we now embrace the *metanoia* (conversion) to a more empowering way of seeing and being? We can identify at least two factors that lead to the popularity of atonement spirituality. First, there is the sense of consolation and strength people obtain from the God who suffers, when they themselves are trapped in poverty or oppression, or on a personal level, confronted by sickness, pain, and the fear of death. The widespread appeal of Gibson's *Passion* shows all too clearly how this lurid fascination can grip people's lives and their search for meaning when faced with the burden and anguish of meaningless suffering.

Second, and more problematic, is the tendency of all patriarchal institutions to foster codependency as a way of exerting
control over the masses. By consistently reminding people of their
sinfulness, their waywardness, and their unworthiness, it is much
easier to evoke compliance, submission, and control. When people
adopt a codependent spirituality, they can easily be cowed into
further submission by highlighting the enormity of their crime
against no one less than Almighty God himself.

Fortunately, people are progressively outgrowing this dysfunctional codependence, although it is still quite common among
fundamentalist Christian groups and seems to be prevalent in
other religious systems as well. Christian scholars throughout the
closing decades of the twentieth century highlighted the problematic and highly dangerous nature of the atonement theory and
its translation into redemptive violence. Translating the inherited
wisdom into an idiom more congenial to our time may not be
sufficient; a more radical reconstruction—honoring the primacy
of the new reign of God (the kingdom)—seems a more authentic
and compelling way to move forward. I return to this topic in
Chapter 9.

Between Calvary and resurrection lies a liminal space in
which women carry out rituals that have been largely overlooked. Kathleen Corley (2010) describes these as funerary rites,
involving grieving, lament, anointing with spices, and stories of
remembrance. Not merely are the women sustained against such
heavy odds, but they are launched into an even more bewildering
space—a more intense darkness—where the first encounters with
resurrection take place. Without the grieving rituals, they might
never have known the empowerment of being raised anew! All the
Gospels make clear that resurrection, in its initial awakening, is a
very frightening space to occupy. The old familiar world has been
shattered to the core. Without the sustenance and empowerment
of collective grieving, it may not be possible to negotiate this dark
night of the soul and the cosmic dawn that promises empowering
liberation.

Christianity has long sought to unravel what exactly happened to Jesus in the experience of becoming the resurrected One, and for much of Christian history, resurrection was assumed to involve the resuscitation of Jesus's dead body, transforming it into a glorified state that defied rational explanation. We need to attend in a more discerning way to what Paul has to say about the resurrection of Jesus. The oft-quoted statement "If Christ has not been raised, then our preaching is in vain, and your faith is in vain" (1 Cor 15:14) is frequently cited without the previous pericope: "But if there is no resurrection of the dead, then Christ has not been raised" (1 Cor 15:13). For Paul, resurrection is a universal archetypal state of deliverance that precedes the death and resurrection of the historical Jesus.[7]

Unflinching commitment to God's new empire cost Jesus his earthly life, in the form of an untimely and brutal death. But we know that was not the end. The first followers—particularly the women—"knew" him to be alive, in fact in a way that intensified and exceeded his earthly mode of human aliveness. That extended aliveness of Jesus we describe as *the resurrection*. What happened to Jesus after his earthly death, we don't know, and at one level it does not matter.[8] What did happen was an archetypal breakthrough, recalling the first witnesses (particularly the women) to God's primary enduring presence throughout the entire cosmic creation.

My personal interest is in the transformation of the followers after the horrendous tragedy of his untimely death. They came

---

[7] Worth keeping in mind here is the already referenced distinction of Richard Rohr between the individual Jesus and the universal Christ: "Christ is God, and Jesus is Christ's historical manifestation in time. . . . Instead of saying that God came into the world through Jesus, maybe it would be better to say that Jesus came out of an already Christ-soaked world" (2019, 15, 18).

[8] It obviously does matter to those who have compiled elaborate treatises on the resurrection of Jesus, such as N. T. Wright in *The Resurrection of the Son of God* (2003). Consisting of over seven hundred pages, the book reviews a wide range of scholarly opinion on the interpretation and meaning of Jesus's resurrection.

through that experience shattered to the core, disillusioned, frightened, disbelieving, and—in the case of the Twelve—scattered far and wide. In time, the liberation of empowerment broke through their anguish. And with Jesus raised from the dead in the power of the Spirit (see Rom 8:11–13), that same empowering Spirit evoked new vision and hope, first in the female followers, and much later in the male ones, leading them to recommit their lives and energy to the work of the God's new reign on earth.

In the case of Jesus's resurrection, I suggest that it is best viewed as the icing on the cake of a life radically lived. It is God's ultimate vindication of the kingdom of God, capturing anew the full cosmic scope of God's radical presence in our midst. Angelic figures, empty tomb scenarios, and various appearances create the metanarrative that empowered early Christian ecclesiology, giving hope and meaning to Christians especially in times of hardship and persecution. However, the glamour and rarity of those events can grossly distract us from the primary goal of Christian faith, which must never prioritize supernatural power from afar for hopeless, passive sinners, but should instead focus on the empowerment born out of the relational matrix of a prophetic person whose life and death were totally devoted to the new reign of God. Only when Christians—and others—take that seriously do we stand any realistic hope of realizing in our own lives what the mystery and meaning of resurrection are all about. From our earthly perspective, it is God's vindication of the beloved ones when we work unstintingly to realize God's kingdom in our earthly, cosmic home.

Let the Paradigm Die!

The paradigm represented in Creation–Fall–Redemption seems to have run its course and served its purpose, despite the fact that millions still adhere to it to one degree or another. As we move deeper into the twenty-first century, a new coming of age, accompanied by novel thresholds of spiritual maturity, registers a substantial rejection of many of its key elements. These include the anthropocentric focus consigning the rest of creation to a subsidiary place; the flawed nature of the human, based on shortsighted anthropological and religious convictions and devoid of evolutionary meaning; an understanding of God that is loaded with metaphysical/patriarchal power-based projections; and a historical reductionism of a few thousand years in a universe of 13.7 billion years, including a human story of some 7 million years. On top of all that, the rescuing interventionist God, who alone can deliver salvation and redemption for humans, undermines the empowering mystery of both God and the human.

For much of Christian history our faith in God, and in Jesus, was based on a religious indoctrination perpetuated by fear-filled patriarchs who believed it was the will of God to keep the masses subdued and uninformed. Worse still, such subservience was obtained by consistently reminding people of their sinfulness and unworthiness. Millions ended up being victims of internalized oppression.

Today, millions are discarding the religious shackles and walking away without guilt or shame. To judgmental religionists, it looks like they are throwing out the baby with the bathwater. To the more discerning eye, I suggest it is people of faith coming of age. While at the overt level, few of those who have walked away seem to be seeking a meaningful alternative, covertly we notice a new spiritual awakening—admittedly chaotic and often confused—with immense promise for a new and more empowering future. My hope is that the theological critique and reframing outlined in this book will help to clarify the evolutionary thrust of what is transpiring at this time.

3

The Imperial Judeo-Christian Paradigm

*Increasingly, followers of Jesus are recognizing that
Christological thinking about him has a "use by" date
that has long passed.*

Lorraine Parkinson

*Jesus's and Paul's vision of a living network of wildly
inclusive, vulnerable communities, grounded in the fullness of love and embodied truth, has been replaced with
institutional fortresses dedicated to keeping out dissent-
ers, with fear-based threats of a judgmental God.*

Wes Howard-Brook

While the previous paradigm worked on three prongs—Creation–
Fall–Redemption—what I will call the imperial approach has five
key elements: Creation–Israel–Jesus–Church–Eschaton. In this
outline, another major religion is brought into play, namely, Judaism. The Hebrew Scripture (Old Testament), while largely eclipsed
in the first paradigm, features strongly in this approach.

Here, we also encounter a tacit acknowledgment of the goodness of Creation, to the extent that it opens up a more dynamic relationship with God, mediated through a group of chosen people in

the land of Israel. However, as we shall see presently, Israel denotes a great deal more than just land, territory, or political identity.

Creation: God's Own Starting Point

Every religious narrative begins with the story of creation, and in several cases the creative flow of the story is interrupted—and distorted—by human interference. Rivalry, violence, and adversarial conflict quickly ensue, and within a short time, the original focus on creation gives way to the problematic of the human condition. The glory of creation is displaced with the inglorious plight of human transgression.

A strange logic then ensues. Human waywardness—in Christian language, sin—expands into a wayward creation, prone to decay, corruption, and death. It sounds like the human has succeeded in corrupting the whole creation, although, in every case, creation preexists the human. This human expansion, often described in anthropocentric terms, seems to be the source and cause of innumerable problems that have bedeviled the human species.

Today, across several contemporary sciences, we evidence a desire to rehabilitate our earth. Ever since Lynn White Jr.'s provocative claim that religion (especially Christianity) has been a primary source of our negative view of creation, we realize that it is not merely Christianity that has contributed to our destructive impact upon the earth (and upon creation at large), but that, indeed, this influence features in several other religious traditions as well. That same dismissive approach has characterized social, economic, and political discourse for several centuries. The human takes priority, to the point where often it seems that only the human matters. All else in creation serves the purpose of fulfilling human need.

This anthropocentric superiority has left us with a damaged and desecrated earth, to a point where human survival is now under serious threat. Evidence is rapidly accumulating to show that without a vibrant and flourishing earth, humans stand little chance of living with dignity and integrity within the planetary-cosmic web of life.

We are only a short step from the theological imperative that God created us as earthlings, and it is in and through a renewed reconnection with earth life that we regain and reclaim our true meaning. But for now, cut off from the earth, we are, indeed, a people in exile (more in Oliver 2020).

The Judeo-Christian narrative begins with the story of creation (especially in Gen 1), in which the mantra "And God saw that it was good" occurs seven times. According to Karen Armstrong (1996, 16), "For the biblical writers, the natural world was not inert and dead. It shared God's own potency, teemed with life, and had its own integrity. When God blessed the earth, he gave the plants, animals, birds, fish, and human beings the power to reproduce themselves so that they too could become creative in their own way."

Central to the covenant (pact) that God made with the people was the gift of an ever-productive land, to be treated with responsible care. However, with the introduction of the original Adam and Eve myth, humans turned the land into a commodity over which they wrangled and fought. From that moment on, the Judeo-Christian myth became ever more violent and exploitive. The power to possess usurped the power of giftedness, and according to Wes Howard-Brook (2010; 2016), the ideology of empire consumed the theology of creation.

For a long time, the theological emphasis has been on the male patriarchal creator who creates ex nihilo. His power is unambiguous, and prior to him nothing exists. He is an ideal projection of the all-powerful ruling male! But Genesis is imbued with a much more subtle and creative life force, which theologians like Jürgen Moltmann, Catherine Keller, D. Lyle Dabney, Whitney Bauman, and Hyo-Dong Lee have been striving to recover. In this contemporary understanding, creation begins not with the Word but with the Spirit. The wind of the Spirit, therefore—the "breath of God"—is that which is constantly bringing us to the realization of our deeply creative universe.

It is in the power of the Spirit that the creative word of the Father is uttered. And this energizing, creative Spirit does not create ex nihilo but out of the depths, the fertile notion of *ex profundis*, so elegantly explained by Catherine Keller, especially in her landmark book *Face of the Deep* (Keller 2003). As I highlight in a previous work (O'Murchu 2011), this insight is not as original as the reader may initially assume. Indigenous peoples have known it for many centuries, encapsulated in their understanding of God as the Great Spirit.

As we shall see in subsequent chapters, our depleted, wounded earth is crying out for redress. Humans are still loath to hear the cry of the earth. Governments are, for the greater part, in a state of denial. Many Christians, still stuck in a dualistic split between the sacred and the secular, don't have an empowering theology or spirituality that would enable them to make more ethical responses. *Theologians are only at the early stages of reclaiming the foundational status of creation as the basis for everything that belongs to God's revelation.* God's first creative gesture, and the unceasing domain of God's benevolent goodness, is in the cosmic-planetary web of life. By failing to make that our authentic starting point, we humans fail to get anything right. Where God begins in time, there too, we must stake our allegiance.

Israel as Symbol

Our human betrayal of God's initial initiative—in and through creation—became institutionalized in the social, political, and economic structures upon which ancient Judaism is constructed. To the fore is the land of Israel, a complex entity that has been the subject of many studies. Originally known as the land of Canaan, it was invaded by the Philistines, Phoenicians, and Egyptians, before famine in the sixteenth century BCE forced the inhabitants to migrate to Egypt. Before the migration, however, a new religious culture came to the fore that was focused on one God only, a belief traced to the great patriarchs (namely Abraham, his son Isaac, and grandson Jacob/Israel). All three patriarchs lived in the land of Canaan, which later came to be known as the land of Israel.

The descendants of Abraham crystallized into a nation around 1300 BCE after their return from Egypt (the exodus) under the leadership of Moses—after forty years in the Sinai desert, he led the people to the land of Israel, understood to be a land promised by God to the descendants of the patriarchs (Gen 17:8). The Jewish monarchy evolved around 1200 BCE with Saul as its first king, followed by David, who made Jerusalem his capital —it would later become the heartland of Jewish worship when King Solomon erected the first temple there around 960 BCE.

First among the three monotheistic religions—Judaism, Christianity, and Islam—Israel symbolized the theology that would dominate the religious landscape for over three thousand years. Genesis 12 highlights the central features: God elects a specific man (Abraham) and a chosen people for a unique redemptive purpose. That election is for the good of all, a plan to save not just Israel but all the nations. Israel understood itself to have been chosen by Yahweh to carry out his will, despite its inherent inferiority relative to the other nations (Num 13:28–29; Deut 4:37–38; Is 60:22). This new arrangement came to be known as the covenant with Israel.

According to this covenant God made Abraham three specific promises:

1. A land chosen (elected) above all other nations.
2. A patriarchal line from Abraham to David and then on to Jesus, through which God's liberation would be delivered.
3. A great "royal" commission, validating the notion of a male-dominated church in New Testament times.

For several Christian scholars, Israel symbolizes a ruling patriarchal God, the one and only true God, who has chosen the people and the land of Israel to be the foundation stone through which God's salvation and liberation will be delivered to all other peoples and nations. Only humans matter in this dispensation, despite frequent allusions to the land and its fertility. Having chosen Israel, God will use its patriarchal rulers (especially the kings) to mediate God's redemptive plan, and when the kings eventually fail, then God's only Son, Jesus, becomes the one who makes the deliverance possible.

Israel and Jesus

Jesus institutes the new Israel, namely the church, to carry forward the divine deliverance. Today, this is a hotly debated issue in which many scholars argue that Jesus's focus is the renewal of the one and only covenant of Israel, fulfilling the deep dreams and hopes of the Jewish people. In this case, the church is just another communal articulation of the covenantal relationship rather than being something uniquely distinctive, meriting a separate (and superior) identity as the Christian Church.

The Jewishness of Jesus is beyond dispute, and certainly his early formative years would have been deeply embedded in the Jewish culture. Since most scholars over the Christian centuries were themselves devoted Christians, they seem to have worked with the assumption (or rather a projection) that Jesus too must have been a devoted religious adherent. As a good Jew, we assume he would have observed faithfully all the details of his religion, just as a good Christian, Hindu, or Muslim would be expected to do. This assumption has become ever more attenuated in recent decades.

Jesus rejected many aspects of his Jewish faith and culture, or more accurately he chose to transcend them.[1] Even with his

---

[1] In the letter to the Hebrews, we are informed time and again that the new covenant embodied in Jesus and his ministry far exceeds the former Jewish covenant: Heb 7:22; 8:6–13; 9:1–20; 10:16–29; 12:18–24; 13:20.

own blood family, relations seem to have been quite strained, as he sought to establish an alternative model of family of a broader and more inclusive frame. By proclaiming and embodying a new reign of God—what the Gospels call the kingdom of God—Jesus was re-creating a whole new way of being in the world, the fuller implications of which are still being discerned by Christian practitioners and scholars alike.

The Gospel writers sought to depict Jesus as a loyal servant of the ruling kingly God, an image the early church councils (especially Chalcedon, Nicaea, and Constantinople) further adorned with metaphysical accolades such as *sovereign, omnipotent, omniscient, infinite,* and *sinless.* They did this in good faith, adopting the widespread belief of the time that God's will for humanity and God's messianic deliverance came primarily through kings, God's primary representatives on earth. Imposing such an imperial prototype on Jesus, and interpreting the messianic expectations of the time from this imperial base, has become increasingly problematic for scholarship (and for millions of Christians as well) throughout the latter half of the twentieth century, as illustrated by such diverse scholars as Wes Howard-Brook (2016), Lorraine Parkinson (2015), Stephen J. Patterson (2014), and John Shelby Spong (2016).

A different quality of Christology is now evolving, with a strong desire to transcend the imperialism of earlier times. And with it comes a growing conviction that the humanity of Jesus, rather than his divinity, is the crucial factor. Jesus, it seems, rejected all imperial posturing in order to become the human face of God made radically visible on earth. And within that same line of Christological argument is a desire to revisit religious adherence to the notion of Jesus as a rebellious, prophetic figure. Can we continue to assume that Jesus followed closely his inherited religion, as most Jews of his day would have done? Or might a contemporary discernment lead us in another direction more congruent with Jesus's vision of a new and empowering companionship between humans and God?

Enter the Church

Did Jesus desire a formalized institutional church in his name? Highly unlikely! What Jesus did desire were small, vibrant, empowering communities, possibly of the type envisaged by St. Paul in his ecclesial basic communities. We glean a sense of their fluidity, flexibility, and creativity from the outline in Acts 2:44–47 and 4:32–37. These communities inhabit a sense of empowerment from the center—primarily to the advantage of the poor and marginalized—and mark a significant shift from a culture of patriarchal domination.

This new egalitarian, anti-imperial dream might well have become the prevailing Christian paradigm, were it not for the huge betrayal of Jesus's empowering vision inaugurated through the Roman emperor, Constantine, in the fourth century. He is largely responsible for adopting Christianity as the official religion of Roman hegemony. The outcome, with its long travail of power and domination, is well captured in the following passage:

> At the very least Constantine, Christianity's first sponsoring emperor, benefited from a theory of incarnation that mirrored his own claims to exclusive status as sole ruler, raising the political currency of his likeness to a divine incarnate image. The imperial church leaders went to great lengths to crown the man from Nazareth with every trapping of royalty and exclusivity, in part, I suggest, because that raised the status and appeal of their faith as well.
>
> In effect, by limiting divine incarnation to a single historical occurrence in the form of Jesus of Nazareth, the council bishops made of Jesus and his mother Mary a beneficent model of dynamic imperial rule. Whatever uncertainties persist about the faith of the Emperor Constantine in his life or at his death bed, his ruthless and bloody drive to become the sole ruler of the known world is well

documented. The development by his bishops of a clear Christology that declared Jesus to be the only begotten son of God certainly gave a divine nod, if not blatant legitimation for the emperor's own goals. Jesus's exclusive filial claim to divinity was made all the more intelligible across the Roman church by widespread patrilineal assumptions about the nature of inheritance. (Laurel C. Schneider, "Promiscuous Incarnation," in Kamitsuka 2010, 241)

For several centuries the church held the balance of power throughout much of the Roman world, with popes and kings vying for superior status. Meanwhile the people of God were encouraged to be loyal and obedient on par with the allegiance of the masses within earthly, imperial regimes. At different times in Christian history, the drive for power oscillated, thus allowing a range of alternative movements to unfold. We note this during what historians sometimes describe as the Dark Ages, namely the Middle Ages, when creative movements like the Beguines, the mystics, and the Franciscans flourished. I wish to suggest that it is from the sixteenth century onward that the clerical imperial domination became a deeply rooted monopoly.

In fact, I suspect that it is after the Council of Trent in the sixteenth century (1545–1563) that things took an ominous twist, with consequences that endure to the present time. It is from Trent onward that the newly separated Catholic Church became a distinctive denomination, initiating a period of clerical domination, legalistic control, and a great deal of irrational fear in the face of any outside challenge. The distorted and dysfunctional coming-of-age that followed Trent morphed into four distinctive categories still visible today: power, devotion, heresy, and altruism.

Clericalized Power

Clerical power became a major issue at the Council of Trent, taking on a central importance also for the other denominations that emerged around the same time: Lutherans, Calvinists, and so on. For Catholicism, the developing emphasis on clerical power was very much a panic reaction. Feeling embarrassed and ashamed by the perceived betrayal of Protestantism, the Catholic Church resolved that it would do everything possible to ensure that such a departure from truth would never again happen.

To that end, the Council of Trent put in place a robust system of structure and regulation to safeguard the one and only truth that the Catholic Church alone could deliver, and created a superior person in charge who is best described by four key words: male, white, celibate, cleric.

Male. Faithful to Aristotle's anthropology, endorsed by St. Thomas Aquinas, only males are considered to be full human beings, with God-given rational intelligence. The other half, females, cannot and must not be trusted with serious responsibilities for the future of the Church.

White. At the time, the white Western world, which essentially means Europe, was regarded as the only civilized part of the planet. The colonization of other parts was already at work in the Americas and in subsequent centuries would spread to other continents. The visions of Trent and of colonization go hand in hand.

Celibate. Since God was viewed as asexual, those who truly represent God must be asexual as well. But there is a further nuance to the celibate state, denoting a quality of holiness equal to God himself. The priest has been granted a divine (or, at least, semidivine) status.

Cleric. Fundamentally, this means a quality of power equal to God himself. So, only a cleric is authorized to speak on God's behalf and to truly represent God on earth.[2]

---

[2] Here we need to note an important distinction between *priest-hood* and *clericalism*. From early Christian times, priesthood was understood as the *servus servorum Dei* [servant of the servants of God] with service as an unambiguous priority. Clericalism is about power, and therefore marks a significant departure from the notion of priestly ser-

With this deadly combination—male, white, celibate, cleric—
no prospect of coming-of-age is tolerated. Even the privileged
clerical few cannot come of age, because they are ensconced in a
regime that is both idolatrous and tyrannical, made up of codependent, dysfunctional relationships. In a sense everybody is pow-
erless, in a system that eventually will implode. However, it can
be so tightly buttressed that it can endure for centuries, eventually
running out of energy, and fragmenting in a rather meaningless
decimation. Evidence for this corrosive fragmentation is visible in
all the Christian denominations today.

Popular Devotion

Those holding the power—the male, white, celibate clerics—
enforced their power chiefly by perpetuating a form of devotionalism that kept people passive, feeling unworthy, obedient,
and subservient. Such devotionalism flourished through various
movements, one of the better known being that of Jansenism.[3]
Original sin was highlighted as the central plight of all humanity,
condemning humans to an enduring state of perversion and sin
that could only be remedied by penance and prayer, in the hope
of making up to Jesus for his cruel sufferings (on the cross) caused
by flawed humans.

One of the major problems with such devotions is that
enough was never enough. The more penance one did, the more

---

vice. Contemporary Christianity, and particularly Catholicism, cannot
hope to resolve its abuse crisis until this distinction is reinvoked.

[3] Named after a Dutch theologian, Cornelius Jansen (d. 1638),
Jansenism was a distinct movement within the Catholic Church
and flourished mainly in France in the seventeenth and eighteenth
centuries. It strongly emphasized original sin, human depravity, the
necessity of divine grace, and predestination. Although explicitly
condemned by Popes Innocent X in 1653 and Clement XI in 1713,
it was endorsed and supported by several Catholic leaders at the
time and also influenced other Christian denominations.

unworthy and inadequate one felt, and therefore, one had to keep adding additional effort. Almost inevitably people began to internalize a tyrannical demanding God who could never be satisfied, a God that would never give the graces necessary for salvation unless we bombarded him day and night.

Such intense pleading with this highly manipulative, punitive God was done through repetitive prayers (e.g., the Rosary), novenas, fasting and other forms of bodily deprivation, pilgrimages, exaggerated use of statues and holy pictures, and frequent attendance at church services. In this way people were kept in perpetual childish immaturity, embracing a sense of faith with little scope for adult growth and development.

In the latter half of the twentieth century many people in the West outgrew the codependency of such devotionalism and in some cases abandoned church practice completely. In other parts of the world, the devotions were integrated with popular fiestas and local community celebrations, and in that process the severity of the penitential practices was reduced considerably. In communities around the world, where poverty and violence prevail, such devotional practices are still prevalent as people hope against hope that God will intervene and rescue them from their awful situations. By upholding and encouraging such devotional practices, instead of confronting on a practical level the systemic injustice and oppression of such peoples, both church and state often collude in keeping the status quo rather than empowering people to push for change.

Heresy and Monolithic Truth

In the post-Tridentine Church, any disagreement with, or deviation from, official Church teaching was automatically marginalizing. There was no room for disagreement or for alternative opinion, and there was no acknowledgment of the hugely diverse nature of faith in early Christian times. There was only one truth, and one way to knowing and appropriating truth, and that was through the teaching authority of the Church.

Theologians were merely mouthpieces for the hierarchy. Theology was strictly reserved to priests and those training for priesthood, a procedure that remained rigidly in place until the second half of the twentieth century. It began to loosen its grip around 1970, when an estimated 5 percent of all theologians in the Catholic Church were laypeople; today it is estimated to be around 60 percent.

During the post-Tridentine period, heresy was not merely about deviating from right doctrine. More significantly, it included breaking the laws and rules in a Church becoming ever more preoccupied with law and canonical regulations, all leading up to the promulgation of the Code of Canon Law in 1917. Law has always been a central feature of Christianity, but with a milder and less extensive application than what happened after the Council of Trent when a new legalistic momentum came to the fore, popularly known as the *Jus Novissimum* (newest law).

Marriage provides a pertinent example. Before the Council of Trent, marriage was not a sacrament in the formal sense. There was a blessing of the union, and concern from the Church for the welfare of spouses and children, but a great deal was left to the people's own initiative in a culture characterized by trust and goodwill. After Trent we witness a gradual movement toward controlling every aspect of people's marital reality, to the present situation in which an estimated one-third of the Code of Canon Law is about marriage.

With more and more people coming of age, heresy has lost much of its historical significance. In several religious and spiritual contexts, laypeople (and nonclerics, such as Sisters) openly question, disagree with, and offer alternative viewpoints regarding official Church teaching. Truth is no longer seen as an ecclesiastical reserve. To the contrary, approximations to truth in the complex world of our time are deemed possible only through a process of multidisciplinary discernment. As I indicate in part two, this way of engaging truth seems far more congruent with the New Testament basis of our faith.

Incarnational Altruism

Despite all the negative factors outlined thus far, suggesting that the post-Tridentine period was one of regression and growing legalism, an incarnational altruism also flourished extensively. Perhaps that will remind us that despite the cultural impositions from on high, a coming-of-age quality endures, particularly among those perceived to be the losers. In religious terms we note this in a range of countercultural movements flourishing throughout the post-Tridentine era.

On the religious front, one movement that has not received the attention it deserves is that of female religious congregations. In 1298, Pope Boniface VIII issued a decree, *Periculoso*, prescribing new and more rigorous standards for the enclosure of women religious than the Western church had previously demanded. The bull reflected current fears that women were inherently passionate and lusted after sexual fulfillment even more ardently than men. At the Council of Vienne in 1311, Pope Clement V extended the *Periculoso* to include Beguines, Tertiaries, and other less formally consecrated women. At a later date, Pope Pius V (1566–1572) declared solemn vows and strict papal enclosure to be essential to all communities of women religious. Such enclosure was never formally revoked, yet a new wave of female religious life emerged in the sixteenth and seventeenth centuries with such pioneering figures as Angela Merici, Louise de Marilac, Mary Ward, and Mary McKillop. They targeted the human and apostolic needs of the poor and marginalized, activating a range of services that were to evolve into the educational systems and health services we know today in many parts of the contemporary world.

Alongside the apostolic congregations of Sisters, a range of charitable services emerged, attending to the medical, social, and educational needs of people, particularly the very poor. Beyond a Church with a public ascetical and legalistic image, there flourished a widespread active devotion, not focused on prayer and penance but on radiating the human face of Christ in compassionate love and empowering liberation. Few historical sources acknowledge this hidden coming-of-age, which sustained millions through pain and struggle.

While historians tend to record the outstanding accomplishments of heroic witnesses, mainly men, and their commanding management of people and resources, the deeper truth of Christian faith belongs to a more complex and largely hidden impetus pioneered by ordinary people, with women playing central roles. In early Christian times, even before Christianity outgrew its Jewish roots, ordinary women, through their homes and families, played significant roles. While the temple and the synagogue was largely controlled by males[4] and managed along patriarchal lines, the household (*oikos*) was characterized by female leadership and initiative. In rural Galilee, this is where the early synagogue meetings took place. It was in such households that Jesus often broke bread with his disciples, with women playing leading roles that, in a few centuries, would become a male reserve. The earliest expressions of Christian faith and flourishing took place in those households. In all probability, it will be through a rediscovery of the household model that the Church of the twenty-first century will flourish anew.

Eschatology: Disillusion or Fulfillment

Finally, I comment briefly on the fifth element mentioned at the start of this chapter: *eschaton*. As already indicated, Paul envisaged a church very different from what we know today. The emphasis was on small, egalitarian communities, with minimal structure and a strong focus on communal empowerment. Paul's ecclesiology,

---

[4] Bernadette Brooten (1982) provides some important information on female rabbis in pre-Christian and early Christian times.

however, was postulated on a short-term endeavor, with a central focus on preparation for God's final in-breaking. It seems that Paul did envisage the "end of the world" to happen in his lifetime—thus, the ecclesial communities served the purpose of keeping people focused on the imminent end and the need to be ready to render an account for their lives.

But the end did not arrive. In fact, since early Christian times there have been many predictions of its arrival, and all have proved to be false alarms. Nonetheless, the notion of a grand divine return to earth followed by a final judgment remains a tenet in several Christian creeds. Christian preachers—and teachers—still promote the notion of an eschatological endpoint,[5] and many of our prayers still allude to the "second coming." Biblically, we vacillate between an apocalyptic doomsday, in which all earthly life will be consumed, and an eschatological breakthrough, after which humans will inhabit something resembling a renewed earth.

Christians who tend to take Scripture literally still adhere to this notion of a final end. For more reflective Christians, and those who bring a critical mind to their faith, the notion meets with wholesale rejection. More informed Christians adopt the challenge posed by Scripture scholar John Dominic Crossan (2010), namely that we need to outgrow the notion of waiting for God's intervention, in favor of an understanding that God is waiting on our collaboration.

The "end" that needs to concern us today—religiously and culturally—is not that of the universe or planet Earth, but that of our own species. If we continue to maraud and commodify the earth, with the intensity and ferocity of modern technology, in just a short few decades we may be sliding deeper into the sixth extinction. That is an "imminent end" that certainly requires a great deal of spiritual and theological discernment.

---

[5] Worthy of note in passing is the observation of Scripture scholar N. T. Wright (2003, 26) that in New Testament studies the word *eschatology* has at least ten different meanings.

4

Progressive Christianity

Beyond Clericalized Theology

*A new Pentecost is stirring in the human soul. Will we
open to this moment of grace and be led into relationships of oneness we could never before have imagined?*
John Philip Newell

*In the depths of every living religion there is a point
where religion as such loses its importance and the
horizon towards which it sets its course permits it to
supersede its particularity and raise itself to a spiritual
liberty that makes possible a new overview of the
presence of the divine in all expressions of the ultimate
meaning of human life.*

Paul Tillich

Part one of this book is an attempt at an overview of how theology has evolved ever since early Christian times. Such a synthesis needs to include a number of theological developments
already unfolding in the second half of the twentieth century.
Among the better known were liberation theology, contextual
theology, feminist theology, multifaith theological discourse, and

the theological interface with new developments in science and cosmology. For the greater part, these were the prerogative of academic scholars, and the ensuing wisdom was largely reserved to an intellectual elite.

Some commentators described these developments as a new theological paradigm, suggesting novel ways of doing theology and engaging the religious imagination. In terms of the present work, I view such developments more as bridges, carrying us across from our inherited theological strategies, as outlined in part one of this book, toward the evolutionary thrust outlined in part two. For instance, liberation theology opened up new vistas of dialogue and interaction with the social sciences, specifically with Marxist analysis. It was mostly studied, however, in Christian universities and in Catholic seminaries, and many of its outstanding proponents were schooled in traditional scholastic methodologies.

Insights from these various new fields spread into the consciousness of the wider Christian community through a range of networks and movements that, viewed in hindsight, were not given the attention and recognition they deserved. They helped to shift the theological consciousness toward the new paradigm that will be outlined in part two of this book. One such network was that of Progressive Christianity, largely a Western phenomenon, but opening up new avenues for theological discernment and discourse that reached well beyond the movement's Western homestead, and beyond the confessional context in which it first emerged.

Currently, the movement consists of a number of organizations, including: the Center for Progressive Christianity (US), the Canadian Center for Progressive Christianity, the Progressive Christian Network (UK); and the Center for Progressive Religious Thought (Australia). The Center for Progressive Christianity was founded in 1996 by retired Episcopal priest James Rowe Adams in Cambridge, Massachusetts. It was established in line with the larger progressive movement within American Christianity taking place in mainline Protestant churches. The center is a nondenominational network of affiliated congregations, informal groups, and individuals.

The Progressive Option

Progressive Christianity (hereafter, PC) is a movement that arose in the latter half of the twentieth century. Its main tenets are outlined on its webpage, www.progressivechristianity.org:

By calling ourselves progressive Christians, we mean we are Christians who . . .

1. Believe that following the path of the teacher Jesus can lead to healing and wholeness, a mystical connection to "God," as well as an awareness and experience of not only the Sacred, but the Oneness and Unity of all life;
2. Affirm that the teachings of Jesus provide but one of many ways to experience "God," the Sacredness, Oneness and Unity of life, and that we can draw from diverse sources of wisdom, including Earth, in our spiritual journey;
3. Seek and create community that is inclusive of ALL people, including but not limited to:
Conventional Christians and questioning skeptics,
Believers and agnostics,
Those of all races, cultures, and nationalities;
Those of all sexual orientations and all gender identities,
Those of all classes and abilities,
Those historically marginalized,
All creatures and plant life;
4. Know that the way we behave towards one another and Earth is the fullest expression of what we believe; therefore we vow to walk as Jesus might have walked in this world with radical compassion, inclusion, and bravery to confront and positively change the injustices we experience as well as those we see others experiencing;

5. Find grace in the search for understanding and believe there is more value in questioning with an open mind and open heart, than in absolutes or dogma;

6. Work toward peace and justice among all people and all life on Earth;

7. Protect and restore the integrity of our Earth and all of creation;

8. Commit to a path of life-long learning, compassion, and selfless love on this journey toward a personally authentic and meaningful faith.

Within these aspirations are a number of more subtle convictions, marking a doctrinal and pastoral departure from an older theology, thus opening up new theological possibilities. One example is that progressives tend to disagree with, and may even be repelled by, the exclusivist beliefs that all religions deem to be important. The unease is with the imperial power games that rumble in the background, and the suspicion that despite all the elaborate claims to divinely revealed truth, several religious tenets are little more than human fabrications, strongly reflecting the dominant culture of one or another historical era.[1] Contrary to the religious denunciation of relativism as one of the great dangers of our age, PC adherents view relativism as the single greatest protection against patriarchal idolatry.

Consequently, the PC movement rejects all claims to the uniqueness of one religion above and beyond all others, or to the evangelistic notion that all spiritual pathways are in error save for one's own. Claims such as biblical inerrancy, established creeds, and church dogmas are viewed as being ideologically rooted in a type of religious imperialism that is no longer sus-

---

[1] Reminiscent of Michel Foucault's "insurrection of subjugated knowledges," in *Power/Knowledge* (Brighton, UK: Harvester Press, 1980), 81.

tainable in our time. In this regard, PC advocates cherish and support the insights of postcolonial religious scholarship (see the overview in O'Murchu 2014) and its penetrating analysis of how colonial indoctrination can survive long after the colonial regime has ended.

PC practitioners seek to be in solidarity with the millions in today's world for whom organized religion has proved ineffectual, irrelevant, or oppressive, as well as with those who have given up on, or are unacquainted with, religious practice. Instead of viewing such people as having abandoned an inherited sacredness, the PC movement seeks to discern in this "prophetic rupture" a search for deeper truth, requiring the clearing away of inherited baggage, or a space to obtain healing from religious indoctrination, guilt, and abuse. The searcher or seeker may be standing on more authentic ground than the one for whom religious faith is clear and certain.

For PC adherents, truth can never be fully possessed, nor can its veracity be upheld in the name of a divinely validated patriarchal power structure (e.g., the church). It is something we pursue with an open and discerning disposition, as we grow more deeply into the emergent wisdom of our evolutionary universe. For members of the PC movement, evolution is simply the way things are, a primary manifestation of divine creativity, keeping life open to the evolutionary surprises that lie up ahead (more in chapter 7) For PC adherents, such an evolutionary perspective also includes a degree of disorder, uncertainty, and ambiguity in life, the paradox of creation-cum-destruction developed in part two of this book.

The evolutionary perspective also invites a different take on morality, namely an *ethic of reciprocity* (Bruni 2008; Maiter, Simich, Jacobson, and Wise 2008; Neusner and Chilton 2008). Relationship defines every evolutionary trajectory, as the creative divine energy seeks out ever deeper possibilities for mutuality and cooperation. This evolving relational web finds its ultimate theological foundation in the doctrine of Trinity (one that is shared by all the major religions), but must never be reserved to humans only. All creatures, planet Earth, and the entire universe are co-participants in this grand cosmic divine/human drama.

For the major world religions, perhaps the greatest stumbling block for the PC movement is its perceived failure or reluctance to take sin and salvation seriously (as understood by the religions). The PC movement begins with the fundamental goodness of all life-forms, humans included, provided we learn to relate rightly at all levels of life. Our inability to get it right is perceived to be not a consequence of an original flaw (original sin, etc.), but of a human failure to honor our God-given status as earthlings. Following the example of Jesus in the gospel project of the kingdom of God, we are empowered to co-create a better world for all life-forms.

The following are some of the names frequently invoked by the PC movement as inspiring sources for the key ideas outlined above: Marcus Borg, John Shelby Spong, John Dominic Crossan, Douglas John Hall, Karen Armstrong, Marilynne Robinson, and Lloyd Geering. Erroneously, the PC movement is often labeled as a *liberal* endeavor supporting the Enlightenment emphasis on rationality as foundational wisdom used to discern truth, very similar to the objectivity required in scientific research. Instead, in most cases, *progressive* denotes a suspicion that formal religious truth has been influenced by a range of extraneous factors, particularly the dynamics of patriarchal power, a distortion requiring a triple corrective: (a) in an evolutionary universe, truth also evolves into ever deeper and fresher understandings, requiring (b) a more penetrating analysis of foundational truths, sometimes described as *reworking the tradition*, requiring (c) contemporary formulations relevant for the evolutionary consciousness of our time—as in the timely synthesis provided by Roger Haight (2019).

The Clerical Shift

As indicated in the previous chapter, a clerical elite—described as the male, white, celibate cleric—emerged from the Council of Trent, with primary responsibility to safeguard authentic truth and ensure that never again would a deviation like the rise of Protestantism afflict the church of Christ. For the next four hundred years (until the 1960s), the male cleric dominated the theological landscape of the Catholic Church—and to a lesser degree, other denominations as well. Only priests, and male students preparing to be priests, had access to Catholic theology. Everyone else was barred.

While such an explicit prohibition does not seem to have existed in the other Christian denominations, the male cleric was at the forefront in the study of Scripture and theology. And with this gender prerogative, theology prioritized the ruling male God in a Church that was overwhelmingly patriarchal in both structure and doctrine. Additionally, there is the Western mind-set, which in the sixteenth century viewed the rest of human civilization as primitive and unenlightened. This gave the priest-theologian an inflated status, not merely in terms of faith, but culture and imperialism as well. Little wonder that Christian theology became so entangled with colonialism.

The following are some of the significant cultural factors that contributed to the emergence of the priest-theologian in the sixteenth century.

1. *Reaction to the rise of Protestantism.* The Council of Trent sought to establish the Church as a kind of impenetrable fortress against any possibility of future error or deviation. The male, white, celibate cleric was to be the key personality in this endeavor.

2. *Colonialism.* Explorations by the Portuguese and Spanish led to European sightings of the Americas (the New World) and the sea passage along the Cape of Good Hope to India in the last decade of the fifteenth century. These expeditions ushered in the era of the Portuguese and Spanish colonial empires, carrying within them an explicit target of Christianizing the lands of the conquered infidels.

3. *The invention of the printing press* around 1455 reinforced new levels of control and orthodoxy. Now that religious truths

and doctrines could be recorded in writing, a new legalism entered all attempts at delivering Christian truth and teaching.

4. *The Renaissance* is a period in European history covering a span between the fourteenth and seventeenth centuries and marking the transition from the Middle Ages to modernity. Responding to the period's new liberalism, expressed in art, music, and other creative expressions, the Christian churches sought to limit the distractions that would lead people away from faith and from the controlling monopoly of the church.

5. *The scientific challenge.* Nicolaus Copernicus (1473–1543) was a Renaissance-era mathematician and astronomer who formulated a model of the universe that placed the sun rather than the earth at the center. This was the beginning of a growing rift between religion and science, with the Christian churches adopting a narrow worldview that would remain largely unchanged until the mid-twentieth century.

Major cultural developments of this type were generally viewed by the Church in a negative light. Reinforced by the dualistic splitting of classical Greek times—earth versus heaven, body versus soul, matter versus spirit—theology was considered to be the sole reservoir of truth, the only wisdom that could explain and deliver God's desire and plan for humans and their world. Humans were the primary concern, the only creatures deemed to be inhabited by a soul, which could only obtain salvation in a world beyond through the mediation of the church, articulated through the power of the Word (in the case of Protestantism) and the sacraments (in the case of Catholicism).

After the Council of Trent, every priest became a virtual theologian in his own right. Only the priest could proclaim the Word, dispense sacraments, and lead souls to the holiness that would assure eternal life. Only priests-to-be were allowed to study theology, and all their mentors were priests. Theology had become a kind of clerical enclave. In turn the priest-theologian was accountable to the bishop, who upon his ordination (as a bishop) automatically became a Doctor of Divinity (DD).

In terms of who does theology, and how it is done, the PC movement marked a subtle but momentous shift from the priest to the layperson. To the best of my knowledge we do not have precise data for this shift. I have not been able to trace a source for the following statistic, which theologians (whom I consulted in the United States and in Europe) consider to be an underestimate rather than an inflated figure: in 1970, 95 percent of all theologians in the Catholic Church were priests (only 5 percent were laypeople); in 2015, an estimated 60 percent of Catholic theologians were laypeople, with 40 percent being priests.

Of the eighty students studying at the International Catholic Institute in Trumau, Austria, in the academic year 2018–2019, six were priests, along with one seminarian; the other *seventy-three* were laypeople. According to the US Center for Applied Research in the Apostolate (CARA), third-level students studying in Catholic institutes rose from 411,111 in 1970 to 769,656 in 2018. African Jesuit theologian Agbonkhianmeghe Orobator (2018, 166) cites the CARA-based figures for lay missionary evangelization in Africa: 393,580 catechists, along with 7,195 lay missionaries, and 928 laymen and laywomen in secular institutes.

The figures serve as mere indicators. What is of greater significance, and extensively borne out by the PC movement, is the shift in theological vision. Whereas the priest-theologian exhibits primary concern for the theological well-being of the church—which in the Catholic context is likely to give preference to sacraments, Catholic morality, authority, and Church history—the lay theologian tends to prioritize the world and the urgent cultural, social, and political needs of our time. For the lay theologian there is an enlarged horizon of engagement, requiring an interdisciplinary mode of discernment, detailed in part two of this book.

Faith Community Reconfigured

The PC movement is not a sect or a cult, and it certainly is not a denomination. In fact, it seeks to transcend the organizational impetus adopted by most of the formal religions. In other words, the primary concern is not to create a new structure or system of creeds, ethics, or religious worship. The envisaged outcome is much more organic, fluid, and flexible, a kind of network through which people can begin to affiliate and mature into the kind of structures that will honor and promote adult dialogue, mutual enrichment, and adult co-responsibility.

Like other contemporary movements, PC may be criticized for placing individual need over community consciousness, a solipsistic kind of salvation over the communal challenge of a church solidly based on the death and resurrection of Jesus. It strikes me that this is a misreading based on an oversimplistic view of the movement. Questioning individuals certainly feature strongly, but they tend to seek a way forward in dialogue and communion with a whole range of others. It is a different approach from what some strands of contemporary spirituality adopt.

The communal dimension remains central and in the forefront. Moreover, it frequently stretches beyond human beings to embrace social, economic, and political systems, as well as the urgent ecological and moral questions facing us today as planetary citizens. This communal focus arises from, and is maintained by, the central role of the new reign of God in the vision and theology of PC, and this aspect tends to be either overlooked or missed altogether by those who are critical of what is unfolding.

Central to PC is the reconfiguration of what we mean by Christian community. It shuns the conformity required by an official creed, ethics, and worship. Seeking to reclaim the earlier notion of *sensus fidelium* (faith of the people), PC aims at religious transformation through *informed, discerning consensus*.

Informed. PC advocates seek a reclaiming of Christian faith employing multidisciplinary research into the cultural conditions in which Christian doctrines were shaped and institutions created, particularly the postcolonial influences that turned Christianity into a religion of empire building. The movement is highly suspicious of the clerical monopoly upholding all the Christian churches.

Discerning. Discernment is the wisdom through which people (not just Christians) seek out what God wants for the evolutionary growth and development of everything in creation. It requires study, reflection, prayer, dialogue, and consensual movement toward empowering action. Orthopraxy, rather than orthodoxy, is the primary goal of Christian discernment ("By their fruits you shall know them," as we read in Mt 7:16).

Consensus. This is a group decision-making process in which group members develop and agree to support a decision in the best interests of the whole. Individually, one may disagree with the final outcome, but based on listening to everyone else's opinion, all the individuals agree to let the decision go forward, because this seems to be the best that the entire group can achieve at the current time. Skillful cooperation is the underlying dynamic, one that is largely unknown in our fiercely competitive world, with few precedents in either contemporary politics or religion.

The Christian Focus

The PC movement, along with the emerging theological culture of our time, is unambiguously Christian in nature, striving to re-create the vision and message of Jesus as perceived to be one of liberating and empowering transformation. The PC movement's primary focus is the new reign of God (the kingdom), perceived to be a global strategy seeking to establish right relationships in the name of love (compassion), justice, liberation, and empowerment.

The PC movement wants to see a refashioned church ever faithful to the new reign of God and not preoccupied with safeguarding its monopoly of power and truth, considered by many progressive Christians to be a serious betrayal of the mission of Jesus and of the power of the gospel. For the movement, the primary task of the church should be the creation and promotion of *liberating and empowering communities* in which everybody has a real say, above and beyond clericalized power and privilege.

The movement has therefore been launched, seeking to support people disillusioned and disenchanted with mainline Christianity. It strongly emphasizes a broad-based faith community inclusive of all, and particularly those who don't measure up to the requirements of religious orthodoxy. It also seeks a close liaison with all Christian denominations and welcomes the enriching interaction of engaging other world religions.

A desire to move beyond the fragmentation and divisiveness often arising from formal religion is one of the primary goals of the PC movement. What unites people is deemed to be more important than what divides. We should prioritize our commonalities, not our divisions. And the desired unity (not to be confused with conformity) is not just about religious believers of the various denominations; it also includes the whole earth and the wider web of life as well, from microscopic bacteria right up through the cosmic creation at large.

Although rarely articulated at length, the movement envisages a sacredness within creation itself—and not merely within people—that merits serious theological reflection, ensuing in a religious practice that embraces the substantial environmental and ecological issues of our time, quite similar to Douglas Christie's notion of a contemplative ecology (Christie 2013). Consequently, an ecologically based commitment to justice is integral to the right relationships envisaged in the movement's central vision.

Many members of PC are affiliated with one or another Christian church, some marginally, others maintaining more regular commitments. Some strive to bring about change from within, and in the process may have been marginalized or even ostracized. Others take a more negative view, believing that due to its long collusion with patriarchal power, the church as we know it today is beyond reform. We need to let it die out so that it can be reborn into something more akin to the global-based, inclusive, and empowering fellowship envisioned by PC.

When seen as a bridge between the earlier confessional models of theology and the evolutionary paradigm described in part

two of this book, the PC movement exhibits several features of
the transitional nature of how people engage their faith today.
Few totally reject the past, even those who are unable to articulate how revival might come about. All, however, are aspiring for
something essentially new, expansive, and empowering. Hopefully,
the reflections in part two can clarify the undercurrents of these
hopes and dreams for a different and better future.

Part Two

Theological Horizons of the Twenty-First Century

What then surely is most new about our modern under-
standing of life is the idea of evolution, for it enables us
to see life not as an eternally repeating cycle, but as a
process that continually generates and discovers novelty.

Lee Smolin

We now take a quantum leap from a time-honored paradigm of almost two thousand years to one that stretches not one but several theological horizons. Even the language looks totally new. The following departure points need to be noted:

- The conventional Judeo-Christian context has largely disappeared; more accurately it has been reframed to a degree that the conventional landmarks—Jesus, gospel, fall, redemption, church, and so on—are so reintegrated in evolutionary terms as be virtually unidentifiable.

- The timescale has been increased enormously. Whereas the Judeo-Christian story tends to be viewed in some thousands of years, we now embrace creation's true story of 13.7 billion years, or possibly even the vast time horizons underpinning the notion of the multiverse.

- The anthropocentric dimension—prioritizing the human—has been reduced significantly. Creation itself comes to the fore with its creative impulse predating humans by billions of years.

- The transpersonal is replacing the personal. The individualized superiority of classical Greek anthropology—projected onto humans and Gods alike—gives way to a relational understanding of personhood, formed and shaped from within the relational nexus of creation itself.

- The notion of God has been radically reenvisioned. Instead of the hierarchical Trinitarian construct, we now prioritizing the Spirit, thus removing the Creator from his imperial, patriarchal throne.

- Continuing the de-throning of the Godhead, Jesus becomes servant to a new global mission, described in the Gospels as the kingdom of God. Personhood, both divine and human, has been recast within a relational, rather than an imperial, mold.

- The Spirit comes to the fore, as suggested in the opening verses of the book of Genesis, and as claimed by indigenous spirituality past and present.

- Theology, as described at one point by Paul Tillich, pursues the ultimacy of God's revelation, no longer gauged by the Judeo-Christian narrative, nor invested primarily in humans, but reenvisioned by the cosmic trajectory of several billion years.

- The apophatic stance of the great mystics is embraced as a safeguard against idolatry. All metaphysical attributes of God—omnipotent, omniscient, impassable—are laid aside, in favor of discerning God at work in the mystery of creation at large.

- Discernment—forever seeking the deeper wisdom of God's Spirit—is our primary theological guide, a process that embraces not merely people of all religions (and none), but also the other creatures that inhabit God's creation with us.

In this outline we are not throwing out the baby with the bathwater. We are—in the best interdisciplinary wisdom of our time—reworking the tradition. However, it is a tradition that is much older and deeper than the inherited wisdom of all formal religions. Tradition is interpreted not so much as clinging on, but rather passing on. And our concern is how best to do that passing on in ways that will honor the evolutionary thrust of deep time, accessed today in billions rather than thousands of years. In this process we hope to ask the right questions and explore the deep recesses such questions open up. Getting to the right questions, rather than providing the right answers (as in the past), is our modest goal.

5

Theology's Paschal Journey

The Paradoxical Imperative

*I once said, perhaps rightly: the earlier culture will
become a heap of rubble and finally a heap of ashes, but
spirits will hover over the ashes.*

Ludwig Wittgenstein

*There is room for all of us in the resurrection conspiracy,
the company of those who plant seeds of hope in dark
times of grief or oppression. Going about the living of
these years until, no one knows quite how, the tender
Easter shoots appear.*

Bob Raines

I wish to begin the second part of this book with a personal narrative. As a writer, this is probably the most daring adventure I have ever undertaken, engaging a paradigm shift involving the collapse of long-held beliefs and the emergence of novel possibilities that shatter many of our former certainties. While I certainly cherish what I have learned from my theological ancestors, I find myself drawn to new horizons inviting me to outgrow the faith that sustained me throughout much of my life. Professionally, I am a social scientist, trying to discern the meaning of evolutionary trends, in this case in theology and Scripture. I am also a rank-and-file Christian in a shrinking ecclesiastical world, but daily encountering spiritual awakenings more congruent with the evolutionary imperative of our time.

I am also the progeny of enlarged scientific horizons that have enamored millions around the world in the past half century, and that influence human perception far beyond most humans' conscious awareness. I consider quantum physics and the new cosmology as foundational to all fields of learning today. Coupled with the information explosion of recent decades, millions of people are now perceiving life in a lateral way that substantially transcends our inherited rational and cerebral modes of engagement. A chaotic creativity inundates the human spirit today that major governments and religious institutions are unable to contain. It feels at times as if everything is falling apart. I suggest that this is *evolution at work*,[1] and as I indicate in the subsequent chapters of this book, I suspect the Spirit will draw forth new life from this breakdown, as has happened in several previous evolutionary epochs.

Which brings me to another resource that hugely influences my discernment: I am a grief therapist, employing a set of skills I acquired several years ago when I worked with people with HIV/AIDS. Not merely do I deal with issues of personal loss and grief, but I apply many of the same insights to the decline and death of systems, organizations, and evolutionary transitions. The basic model I adopt is the one developed by renowned psycholo-

---

[1] Worth keeping in mind here is that evolution is not something we can manage and control, but rather something that happens to us: "We ourselves are being changed," writes Thomas Berry in "The Divine and Our Present Revelatory Moment," in Thomas Berry, CP, and Thomas Clark, SJ, eds., *Befriending the Earth: A Theology of Reconciliation between Humans and the Earth* (Mystic, CT: Twenty-Third Publications, 1991), 4–7.

gist Elisabeth Kübler-Ross, outlined in five stages: denial, blame (anger), bargaining, depression, and acceptance (Kübler-Ross 1969). From within this background I engage the notion of the paschal journey with a newness full of paradox but also one of profound hope.

As a grief therapist, I am acutely aware of the huge resistances we employ when faced with terminal life issues, whether in daily loss, sickness, or death. We dread insecurity, endings, and finality, and most of us feel very uncomfortable with vulnerability, weakness, or the need to let go. These resistances are not just part of the human condition. They become more deeply ingrained in us because of the patriarchal indoctrination to which many of us have been subjected. According to this indoctrination, God is in charge, and so are the human forces that God has chosen. Through the power of rational reason, incorporated into our faith, we can keep chaos and disintegration at bay. And with the reassurance of our faith, we know we can conquer the obstacles of human weakness, including death, the great enemy that thus far only Jesus was able to subdue.

Our human vulnerability today is further exposed as we confront the issues of earth's depleting resources and our human collusion with environmental fragmentation. For most people it is business as usual, but subconsciously our confidence has been shaken and our place as earthlings is becoming increasingly uncertain. In many cases this reinforces the defenses we erect to keep chaos at bay.

Every therapist has encountered these resistances. Common sense alone will indicate how much more recalcitrant they become in the social and religious systems that frame our lives. To this end we tend to sanction and solidify human structures, which over time become permanent institutions, impervious to change or alteration. Philosopher-economist Charles Eisenstein perceptively notes the immortal values we have inscribed into our capitalistic economic system. While everything in the natural world undergoes dying and revitalization (more accurately: death as a prerogative for new life), not so our money system. We don't set a life limit on our notes and coins, or the electronic value of our cash. We have made our money immortal, treating it like a god. Eisenstein opines that most of the financial headaches bewildering our world today could more easily be rectified if we allowed our money to die, like everything else in nature going through the cycle of birth-death-rebirth (more in Eisenstein 2011, 203ff.).

In this chapter I briefly review how we employ a dynamic of change, decline, and death in our engagement with Scripture and theology. We seek permanence and fixity in doctrines and dogmas that are intended to last—in some cases forever! While we wax eloquently about the paschal journey in spiritual literature, or on occasions such as funerals, we fail to apply it to those many life experiences of fragility, vulnerability, and letting go. When it comes to death itself, we have religiously declared it to be an evil to banish. Perhaps right there is where we need a new theological horizon, one that honors and embraces the meaning and necessity of death, even within the sacred precincts of theology itself.

The Paradoxical Imperative

As a grief therapist I feel a great sadness every autumn as I watch the leaves turn brown and gradually fall to the ground, leaving the trees with a bare and barren look. And I am quickly reminded of the paradox of all creation: birth-death-rebirth, or as outlined by cosmologists Brian Swimme and Thomas Berry (1992), the recurring cycle of creation-cum-destruction. If those trees do not shed their leaves and become totally bare, then we will not have a subsequent spring bursting with new foliage, full of life and vitality. The dying of the autumn time seems to be a prerequisite for the vitality of spring—death and resurrection at work in creation itself.

Long before Jesus ever underwent death and resurrection, it was already occurring throughout the entire universe. In a previous work (O'Murchu 2011, 165), I write,

While many disciplines, religious and secular, deem the paradox to be an aberration of a sinful and deranged world—or more accurately, out of balance because of human fickleness—I believe we need to see it afresh and reclaim it anew as an integral aspect of creation in its emerging growth and development. God's creativity is in the destruction and death as well as in the birthing forth of novel and emergent forms.

Paradoxically, the same Spirit who can be fierce and bewildering explodes in the cacophonous disintegration which occurs extensively in the galactic realm, in the elegant and painful death of stars and the sometimes violent dispersal of stellar debris. This process can also be described as the unceasing cycle of birth-death-rebirth. This is not a deviation, but an inherent aspect of the wisdom within which all life unfolds, develops and endures. In religious language it is a divinely bestowed aspect of universal life (not to be confused with intelligent design), and therefore not an evil to get rid of. Rather it is a paradox to be embraced and befriended and, in that way, transformed into a powerful evolutionary force without which everything would cease to be.

It is one of the oldest dynamics known to universal life. The process of death-cum-resurrection did not begin with Jesus of Nazareth; rather the historical Jesus, being a person of cosmic significance, underwent in his own life the paschal journey that underpins everything in creation. That creative immolation is not some type of satanic anomaly, but a grace-laden endowment of divine beneficence.

We are dealing with paradox, which takes us beyond the sphere of rational discourse and scientific objectivity. We can understand *paradox* as *a contradiction with meaning written underneath*. Like the Gospel parables, the meaning is hidden and has to be uncovered. We encounter the paradox in a phrase from

St. Paul (2 Cor 12:10): "When I am weak, then I am strong." In our daily experience of life, strength and weakness are polar opposites, and the former is the one we all relish. Many of us, however, can recall moments in life in which we encountered the paradox; failure or sickness carried a paradoxical message inviting us to make life changes guaranteeing a better future.[2]

All over creation this paradoxical process is at work. Without it, life as we know it would cease to be. In the outer realms of space-time there are continuous cacophonous collisions, an integral dimension of coming to birth for galaxies and planets. The earth's tectonic plates are forever shifting, releasing pent-up energies so that the earth's body can function more dynamically; every now and again, this results in earthquakes. Religionists sometimes suggest that God causes the earthquake as punishment for the people's lack of faith. In truth, the earthquake itself is a dimension of divine co-creativity; without earthquakes we would have no earth nor the elegant array of life-forms we encounter each day.

So, throughout creation, there is the paradoxical imperative of birth, death, and rebirth. It is a divine endowment, and fortunately we humans cannot get rid of it no matter how hard we try. It is crucially important that we accept the paradox as divinely bestowed and not view it as some mere freak of nature. With such acceptance, we stand a better chance of discerning more authentically two of life's great quagmires: the significance of suffering and the meaning of death.

The Christian religion, in conjunction with several faith systems, views suffering in the world as the fallout from human sin. The onetime harmonious creation has ever since been distorted,

---

[2] I am reminded of a book by a controversial Australian doctor, John Harrison, *Love Your Disease: It Is Keeping You Healthy* (Sydney: Angus and Robertson, 1984). The example frequently cited is that of a dose of flu that requires one to take to bed for a number of days. He suggests that this experience can be interpreted as your body telling you that it needs to be in bed for a number of days. The sickness carries a paradoxical message for a heathier way of living.

and will remain so, until the end of time, when all will be set right again in God's eschatological accomplishment. The death and resurrection of Jesus took the sting out of suffering but did not get rid of it. *This line of argument makes no sense in an evolutionary universe.* There has never been a perfect idyllic time, nor is there likely to be some grand finale at the end of the world.

An important distinction arises here, namely between meaningless suffering and that which is necessary for evolutionary growth and development. Several years ago, French philosopher Paul Ricoeur and Irish theologian Gabriel Daly each suggested that most of the meaningless suffering in the world is actually created by us humans. Therefore, meaningless suffering is primarily a human problem, and not a divine one, and a major aspect of that problem is our appalling ignorance about the paradoxical nature of the universe we inhabit. We don't know how to engage meaningfully with paradox because we are unable to discern its significance in the first place. It is inappropriate, therefore—indeed irresponsible—to be looking to the crucified one on the cross to rescue us from the mess that we ourselves have created.

A related topic is that of death, the meaning of which largely escapes us, indoctrinated as we are with the religious notion that it is an anomaly we need to get rid of. Here we run into major conflict with the teaching of St. Paul, who categorically asserts that death is the consequence of sin (cf. Rom 6:23). Death existed long before human sin ever came into the picture. Our ancestors have long known that death is integral to universal life, and in several ancient cultures the current phobia around death and dying did not prevail. We must come to understand death as a divinely bestowed phenomenon, central to the paradoxical process of creation-cum-destruction. If the autumn leaves don't die out, there will be no "risen" foliage next spring. Without such dying and diminution, evolution comes to naught.

Death is a prerequisite of new life, evidenced across the entire web of organic life-forms. As with suffering, we need to distinguish what constitutes meaningless suffering from those forms that are required by divine evolutionary necessity. And the pursuit of a more responsible way of dealing with dying and death needs to become a human prerogative in which we transcend the centuries-long codependence on a rescuing risen Savior. We need to commit fully to the evolution of life, just as Jesus did, and when we do that, we too might have to pay the prophetic price of an untimely death. As for the resurrection of Jesus, instead of viewing it as a miraculous divine resuscitation of a dead corpse—which is really a Godless, blasphemous claim—we need to reenvision the risen empowerment as a feature of the first disciples picking up where Jesus left off, and continuing to build on earth the new reign of God.[3]

We Are the Sixth Extinction

Our irrational fear of death, and our elaborate religious theories that both demonize and seek to transcend it, actually feed the huge cultural confusion in which humanity finds itself today, exemplified so vividly in the COVID-19 pandemic. On the one hand, we live out of an inflated anthropology, convinced that we are the superior species with a divine right to lord it over everything else in creation. And that inflated ideology—and the theology that sought to validate it—has now reached a breaking point in the havoc we are creating as deranged earthlings.

In 1995 Richard Leakey and Roger Lewin coauthored a book titled *The Sixth Extinction: Patterns of Life and the Future of Humankind.* The authors revisit the five previous major extinctions[4] that seriously depleted organic life at the time, and they go

---

[3] In a previous work, I argue that the first disciples were not merely Peter and the Twelve, but primarily Mary Magdalene and her coworkers (O'Murchu 2015, chapters 11 and 12). More on this later in the present volume.

[4] The five are usually named as the End-Ordovician, Late Devonian, End-Permian, End-Triassic, and End-Cretaceous, the first occurring about 440 million years ago, and the last 66 million years ago. The

on to highlight what is increasingly looking like a sixth major extinction, largely brought about by humanity itself. Almost twenty years later, the grim prognostication is much more rigorously outlined in a similarly titled work by Elizabeth Kolbert (2014). This time around, humans are driving many life-forms to virtual extinction, largely oblivious to the fact that we ourselves cannot survive on a planet where organic diversity has been so diminished.

As we move deeper into the twenty-first century, climate change and global warming evoke major concern for the human species despite the fact that a number of world governments (including China and the United States) ignore or dismiss the scientific evidence. The problem facing humanity is a great deal more complex since the warming in question is driven by a range of factors not subject to human control. In fact, several evolutionary breakthroughs have been fueled by climate change, of either extreme heat or extreme cold. Never before, however, have humans been so directly involved, and with such destructive impact. Our misguided interference arises from a number of related factors, of which monotheistic religion is a central feature: (1) humans claim a God-given right to rule and dominate the earth; (2) the earth itself, understood to be fundamentally flawed, is a commodity for human use and benefit; and (3) the earth represents the dualistic secular realm, perceived to be at variance with the holiness of the sacred—it is the vale of tears for which religion has long offered an escape route.

Consequently, all organic processes marked by decay and death are viewed negatively as features of the fundamental flaw that characterizes all creation; *flaw* and *paradox* are grossly confused in this framework. And humans end up perpetuating an inflated anthropology, first setting ourselves over against, and

---

evolutionary significance of these events was first outlined by D. Raup and J. Sepkoski Jr., "Mass Extinctions in the Marine Fossil Record," *Science* 215, no. 4539 (March 19, 1982): 1501–3.

superior to, the natural world, and second, assuming that with the aid of grace from the imperial God, humans themselves can help conquer the mess, and eventually eliminate the curse of death.

Today we are called to a very different type of conversion, requiring the kind of theological foundations outlined in this book. First and foremost, we live within an ecology (an ecological system). Our society and economy rely entirely on that ecological system. Our economy at best is an abstraction based upon our ecological reality, but sadly it has developed its own systemic logic that contradicts both ecology and basic physics.

Describing our economic plight, theologian William Cavanaugh writes,

> Economics does not just suggest other ways of acting in the world, but presents an alternative vision of "ultimate reality." It is commonly recognized that academic economics has grown from ecclesiastical roots, from the Reverend Malthus at the beginning of the nineteenth century to social gospeller Richard Ely—founder of the American Economic Association—at the end of the century. Original Sin was replaced by an original competition over scarce goods. The salvation story is that economic progress would save the world. . . . Adam Smith's idea of the "invisible hand" of the market is not that there is an ethic of self-interest embedded in neoclassical economics, but rather that such economics serves as a type of theodicy that explains how divine providence turns evil into good. Money occupies the place that God once occupied in Christian society. (2016, 67–68)

In earlier capitalism a family could own a single store, farm, workshop, or factory and keep it as their subsistence business for generations without a need for continuing expansion. However, with the rise and dominance of global corporations, we have become enmeshed in a fraudulent scheme of shareholder profit maximization that has produced a flawed dependence on continual economic growth, on a finite planet. Today humanity is enduring a massive paschal journey, carrying the cross of inflated dysfunctional economics, fueled in several cases by corporate greed and planetary exploitation. If Christianity stands any hope for future credibility it must outgrow its narrow anthropocentric notions of salvation and redemption and recognize the corporate, political, and economic crucifixions of our time.

Christ's Death and Resurrection

Christian theology has long assured us that all will be well, as Jesus has resolved the great paradoxes of life in his own death and resurrection. Today, this belief creates a false utopia based on a set of theological assumptions that have lost much of their credibility. In chapter 2 I outlined the broad strokes of how the death and resurrection of Jesus were viewed in early Christian times, particularly under the influence of St. Paul. The focus rests primarily on the human flawed condition, which needed a divine resolution that could only be achieved by the death and resurrection of the historical Jesus.

Most Christians still adopt this understanding, but not all. As we discern more deeply the empowering mission of Jesus (via the rubric of the kingdom of God, see chapter 9), it becomes much clearer that Jesus was killed by the religious-imperial forces of the Romans-cum-Jewish authorities of the day, because he posed such an enormous threat to their power. As the followers became healed and empowered, the powers that be at the time felt they had to get rid of the subversive empowerer (Jesus, in this case), and they did it by the method most commonly used to eliminate subversives, namely crucifixion.

The twelve apostles fled (at least most of them), lest they too be crucified. Those who stayed, seeing Jesus through the traumatic end of his life, were Mary Magdalene and her companions, a female-led group, but in all probability consisting of both women and men, as Cynthia Bourgeault avers (2010, 252n1). The persistent fidelity of these women is one of the most neglected elements in our understanding of the primordial paschal journey. Quite rightly Elizabeth Johnson invites us to a deeper discernment when she writes,

> The presence of the women at the Cross has historical warrants. All four Gospels agree that a group of women kept vigil, standing firm in the face of fear, grief, and the scattering of the male disciples. Women standing at the Cross, or at a distance, kept the death watch, their faithfulness a sign to Jesus that not all relationships had been broken, despite his feeling of intense abandonment, even by God. . . . The fact that they are mentioned in every Gospel eloquently strengthens the argument that their presence at the Cross is historically accurate in general outline. (2003, 294)

What sustained those women through such pain and trauma? Why did they stay on, faithful until the end, when so many others had fled? In all probability, it was their wisdom and skill at ritualizing their loss, anguish, and trauma. They resorted to mourning the departed one through a range of lamenting chants, dirges, and ceremonies of anointing. "Women were also the ones who enacted the majority of funerary rituals all over the Mediterranean world. The funerary rituals were often held in corporate groups and associations, and Christians were no different from their pagan neighbors in their celebrations of mourning throughout the year and on special holidays on which the dead were honored and remembered" (Corley 2010, 20). The women were adept and skillful at this task, one often misunderstood and dismissed as morbid and primitive. What is employed here is an ancient wisdom of entering deeply into grief and loss, and by such ritualized engagement, the participants were able to walk through the depths of sorrow into the light of greater hope for the future. What we are witnessing, as elaborated by scholars such as Kathleen Corley (2002; 2010), is a deeply spiritual process that is both liberating and empowering.[5]

Jan Assmann, formerly professor of Egyptology at the University of Heidelberg, claims that the restoration of the body after death is a female preoccupation in several ancient cultures. The means that are utilized for restoration include lamentation, mourning, affective language, and expressions of desire and longing. The ritual aims at recollecting the scattered limbs and restoring the dismembered body. Female mourning is concentrated on the bodily sphere of the dead—not as an end in itself, however, but as a liberating transformation. The Gospel women did not flee the awful scene of Jesus's crucifixion, and by enduring that dark night they become the first to witness the empowering breakthrough that Christians name as resurrection. Befriending the dark night is thus an essential dimension of engaging authentically with the empowering rising to new life theologically described as resurrection.

Scripture scholar Walter Brueggemann offers several perceptive insights into this paradoxical empowerment, which those Gospel women evidenced so profoundly:

> Only grief permits newness. . . . Where the grief is silent, the newness does not come and the old order survives another season. . . . Jesus' main conflict is with the managers of the

---

[5] Kathleen Corley, in her masterly work *Maranatha: Women's Funerary Rituals and Christian Origins* (2010), goes on to make the bold claim that the original versions of the passion story, the oldest part of the Gospel narrative, evolved from the storytelling that accompanied the grieving rituals: "Rather than being exclusively a scribal product and originally a written document from a subculture dominated by well-educated men, as virtually all scholars suppose, I am suggesting that the passion narrative had its origins in a grassroots liturgical context dominated by women and ordinary people. Thus, its origins are in an oral genre found among ordinary people who visited the grave sites of their loved ones and sang—and sang again—the stories of notable deaths in their community, in this case Jesus. It is women's laments that lie at the heart of the narrative core of the passion story" (128).

old order who do not know of its failure and who will
do whatever is necessary to keep the grief from becoming
visible. For if the grief does not become visible then the
charade of the old order can be sustained indefinitely—and
newness will never come! If the hurt is fully expressed and
embraced, it liberates God to heal. (1986, 41, 44)

Not merely do the women make the grief visible, they integrate it into their paschal journey, and it liberates them to move
through the dark night to the breaking dawn of new life.[6]

Through the story and experience of those Gospel women,
we are invited to reconstruct the paschal journey of our faith as
a Christian people. It is unlikely that the group of twelve men following Jesus were key players in this traumatic event. The liberating and empowering praxis belongs primarily to Mary Magdalene
and her co-disciples, a grossly neglected dimension of our inherited
faith. Worse still are the neglect and suppression that followed. One
wonders if there was not a deliberate attempt to erode from history
the very people who laid the foundations for what was to become
the Christian Church. Thus, historian Mary Malone writes,

For about 25 years immediately after the death and resurrection of Jesus, the small new Christian community
was a fully inclusive community. It seems to have originated from the initiative of women. After the men had

---

[6] In the case of Mary Magdalene, generally considered to be the
inspiring leader of that group of disciples, Cynthia Bourgeault (2010)
captures what that breakthrough means: "And so it is on the morn-
ing of Resurrection . . . she is the last person he sees before he leaves
the human realm and the first person he sees upon returning. Together
again, in that garden where life and resurrection have become a single
flowing river, they once again gaze into each other's eyes, exchanging
their unspoken joy. Then, with a forceful, 'Go and tell the others,' he
sends her forth from the bridal chamber to take up her post as a cosmic
servant" (156).

"abandoned him and fled" the women disciples remained faithful. They gathered together the scattered remnants of the traumatized followers of Jesus and melded them into a functioning, and eventually missionary group. These first 25 years seem to have been years of a feverish activity, with women and men apostles, prophets, teachers, and preachers racing up and down from Jerusalem, spreading the Good News. By about the year 55 CE a discriminatory trend set in. . . . The community that had been initiated by Jesus and carried on by the women was now reverting to a patriarchal model. For about another hundred years, there are signs of a struggle, but by the end of the second century, a male-dominated Church was settling into place. (2014, 167)

Why was that initial women-led enterprise subverted—in fact, completely crushed—within a short period of time? From the letters of 1 and 2 Timothy, Titus, and 1 and 2 Peter, we can glean a concerted and persistent move toward a predominantly male, hierarchical church, but there is widespread agreement among scholars that those letters were written after 100 CE. Mary Malone's outline of a dominant female movement is now regaining favor among a growing body of contemporary scholars, although few can explain what led to the original derailment of that empowering initiative.[7]

Controversial and heretical though it may sound, I want to suggest that in all probability the group known as the Twelve did *not* return, certainly not all of them! The Twelve did not undergo

---

[7] The most convincing explanation I have encountered is that of the American Scripture scholar James Carroll (2014), who attributes the suppression to the Roman-Jewish War of 66–72 CE. Consistently, women (and children) have been the greatest victims of war, and the disempowerment of the early Christian women-led enterprise also seems to have been disenfranchised in a significant way by violent suppression of the Roman-Jewish War.

the paschal journey and consequently were unable to embrace the dark, fertile dawn that followed. In Acts 2:1–4, Luke reassembles the reconstituted group of twelve; he needs them reassembled to lay solid apostolic foundations for his two great heroes, Peter and Paul, but how historically (or theologically) reliable is this assumption? The serious dilemma that ensues is well captured by Elizabeth Johnson (2003, 300) in these words:

> Desiring to impress his readers in the Roman Empire with the trustworthiness of this new movement, Luke consistently depicted men in public leadership roles and, in order to conform with the empire's standards, kept women decorously under control in supportive positions. Having eyes mainly for elite men, he fudged women into an insignificant background ignoring the leadership roles they in fact held. . . . Consequently, Acts does not contain a representative picture of church leadership in the early decades. It tells only part of the story.[8]

And the part it tells leaves us in a historical and theological vacuum that is now returning to haunt Christianity. The paschal journey that the foundational males evaded must now be undertaken by both males and females of our time. Death and dying are all around us, in every sphere of contemporary religion. Let's not run away this time but seek the grace to stay with the darksome deep, because as happened two thousand years ago, that is where the primordial awakening of resurrection is most likely to transpire.

---

[8] For a more up-to-date overview on how contemporary scripture scholars view and assess Luke's treatment of women, see Barbara Reid, "The Gospel of Luke: Friend or Foe of Women Proclaimers of the Word," *Catholic Biblical Quarterly* 78 (January 2016): 1–23, based on a talk given at the Catholic Biblical Association of America in August 2015.

Religion's Paschal Journey

As a world religion, Christianity carries a great deal of baggage that needs to be shed. It is not one but several "Calvarys" that need to be endured. And without letting go of past constructs—which, at one time, may have served us well—we cannot hope for a genuine religious or theological revival. The following are some of the cultural presuppositions that served us in the past but for the future could present huge barriers to new life.

- A static, time-constrained worldview with the two-thousand-year benchmark carrying exaggerated importance, with little or no sense of evolutionary becoming across more expansive time horizons. The God who co-creates over billions of years has been reduced to an earthbound agency of a mere few thousand years.

- A human anthropocentric context that inflates the human and consigns the rest of creation to relative insignificance. Only humans really matter, and consequently all the major religions exhibit a range of human projections that distort and undermine the true Godly value of all other aspects of creation.

- All the religions adopt patriarchal power as the assumed God-given mode of governance and guidance. The God figure at the head of the hierarchy is typically male and "all-powerful," often described as a ruling king, and loaded with imperial projections.

- While mainline religion seeks to establish and facilitate a personal relationship with the divine One, the underlying anthropology—and the consequent understanding of the personal—are not relationally grounded. Therefore, instead of the inherited notion of being formed in the image and likeness of God, we invest an enormous amount of religious rhetoric and piety molding God into our anthropocentric image and likeness.

- While the doctrine of the Trinity supports the notion of a relational deity, most Christians view God in narrowly individualistic categories, within a hierarchal framework of Father–Son–Holy Spirit. Jesus is often viewed in isolation as the great divine rescuer, and the Holy Spirit is a nebulous third entity largely ignored for most of Christian history.
- The notions of salvation and redemption, articulated through the theory of atonement, instead of reducing the "evil" in the world have probably exacerbated it, in the sense that they leave humans off the hook in terms of addressing the wrongs for which we, and not God, are responsible.
- Postulating truth in terms of indisputable sacred texts, many of which are heavily enculturated, no longer works in a world of mass information. Consensual dialogue is considered to be a more reliable method to generate approximations of truth.
- We need to outgrow the practice of dualistic splitting, so that we can integrate the sacred and the secular, particularly in reference to our own status as earthlings (more in Oliver 2020).

If the above describe some of the major letting-go dimensions, what we need to die to in our theological paschal journey, then what are some of the new awakenings—intimations of resurrection—that call forth our discerning wisdom?

- As a species we need to learn the art of grieving so that we can liberate ourselves from the dead weight of congealed systems and outdated understandings, thus empowering us to engage more fruitfully in the evolutionary awakenings of our time.
- We need to take as normative the enlarged and ever-deepening worldview as outlined in the new cosmology and in quantum physics.

- We need to embrace an anthropology based on our true human story of some 7 million years and not the reductionistic paradigm of merely recent millennia.
- We need to adopt an apophatic spirituality whereby we strive to live in more God-like ways, rather than theorizing about the Godhead.
- Let's do justice to our Christian story so that we prioritize the new reign of God (see Mt 6:33) and situate the historical Jesus as the primary disciple of that dispensation rather than modeling his life and ministry on imperial domination.
- We need to rehabilitate the Holy Spirit as the primary manifestation of the divine in our earthly-human awareness, and as the first intuitive and mystical insight into the meaning of God.
- We need to remove God the Father from the imperial throne and substitute a creative life force, of more maternal significance, congruent with the notion of the ancient Earth Mother Goddess.
- We need to reimagine and reenvision our understanding of church, with primary emphasis on empowering local communities (like Paul's ecclesial groups) in which laypeople, and not clerics, are the primary animators and facilitators of prophetic word and inspiring sacrament.

Continuity and Tradition

Engaging the paschal journey, in this time or in any other, requires an enormous depth of discerning wisdom. The decline of Christianity and of Christian influence around the world cannot be attributed merely to secularization, postmodernity, or rejection of religion. The decline of patriarchal religion arises from internal corruption and cannot be blamed on external attack. A range of internal factors mark the disintegration of Christian faith in our time. The faith itself is in crisis, not merely because of external adversarial forces, but primarily because of internal malaise and corruption. The faith system itself is in terminal decline, and the only long-term resolution is to undergo its paschal journey, the dying that is a precondition for the refounding of new life.

I have already outlined the aspects that need to die, which are focused mainly on patriarchal power. For those seeking to preserve authentic tradition and a sense of continuity, a number of issues need to be clarified. Continuity of tradition is not a linear process, a straight line from a point of origination up to the present moment. Several years ago, American biologist Niles Eldredge (1985) described evolutionary growth in terms of punctuated equilibrium, significantly different from the neo-Darwinian emphasis on survival of the fittest by building on that which endures from the past. Eldredge reminds us of the great extinctions, in which the leading life-forms of the time suffered serious decline and were replaced by forms that were essentially new (e.g., replacing the dinosaurs with birds, who share over a hundred distinct anatomical features with theropod dinosaurs; in more recent times, frogs are considered descendants of the dinosaurs).

The course of evolution evidences death and resurrection at work. At a deep level, continuity prevails, but it is subtle and not congenial to human rational analysis. On the surface there are several moments of discontinuity, like the tree shedding its autumn leaves. Christianity as we know it today clings to several elements that are peripheral rather than essential, for example, the allegiance to patriarchal power, the literalization of Scripture, atonement theology, the notion of an interventionist God, Aristotelian-based anthropology, and dualistic splitting. As we peel away the layers of colonial posturing, we come to another view of Christian faith, epitomized in the Gospels as the kingdom of God. This seems to be the fundamental blueprint, which translates into a range of cultural and religious possibilities as circumstances demand. Viewing our Christian faith in this evolutionary, organic way does not undermine the authentic tradition; to the contrary, it roots it more deeply, as we seek to honor the foundational, empowering liberation of Jesus rather than the imperial framing that has been adopted for much of the past two thousand years.

Who then decides what constitutes authentic truth? We see evidence in the world today of a widespread skepticism around all forms of patriarchal authority, secular and religious alike. For the most part, I think this is a healthy development, one that empowers us to engage more authentically with the paschal journey of faith in our time. Much more challenging is the emerging disillusionment around academic research as well, as centers of academic learning seem to be overly devoted to their own self-perpetuation. An alternative vision is coming to the fore—seeds of a new resurrection—in wisdom from the ground up, as more and more people, influenced by our culture of mass information, ask penetrating questions, express doubts and reservations (on almost everything in life), and seek responses that engage their own wisdom and imagination.

This new forum for truth is named by Scripture scholar Walter Brueggemann as that of communal obedience (*obaudiere* = to listen attentively): "But the Church, with its excessive penchant for dogmatic certitude, and the academy, with its fascination with objective rationality, characteristically stop short of the evidence of communal obedience" (2005, 9). No one person, no one structure, has access to ultimate truth. Rather, we reach toward deeper truth as together we discover new ways of contemplative listening, dialogical skill, and the art of consensus making (all of which I elaborate on in an earlier work, O'Murchu 2019). For some this is perceived as a collapse into relativism, with all sense of absolute truth undermined. The process of communal obedience is certainly not about absolutes, nor can it be dismissed as relativistic. Rather, it offers a new modality for seeking truthfulness, congruent with the evolutionary imperative of our age.

The revival of Christian faith in the contemporary world is not dependent on demonizing the forces of postmodern secularism, nor is it dependent on returning to a pure version of the truth (tradition) that endures come what may. What is at stake, instead, is a kind of purification process—clearing away the clutter and debris (as earthquakes do for planet Earth)—so that the more authentic foundations become clear once again, and can be rehabilitated in a manner that is congruent with the evolutionary imperative of our age. In a word, we need to engage a dying and letting go of much that we cherished—in some cases for almost two thousand years—so that we free up the energy flow for the Spirit to re-create as the Spirit has so often done throughout the long eons of evolutionary becoming.

In terms of the paschal journey, the new evolutionary horizon is not so much about revisiting the notion of resurrection, whether in terms of Jesus or of the postulated general resurrection of all humans at the end of time. Instead, I suggest, we need to engage afresh with that energizing and empowering Spirit, source and foundation of all that rises to new life.[9] That inspiring and empowering horizon is our discerning task for the next chapter.

---

[9] Recall Paul's assertion in Rom 8:11 that it is in the power of the Spirit that Jesus is raised from the dead.

6

The Originating Spirit

*The life-giving power of the Spirit who empowered
all creation is also the power of resurrected life for
all beings.*

Elizabeth Johnson

*A Church that seeks to follow where the Spirit leads
will have to expect the unexpected and be prepared to
be shaken to its core.*

James G. D. Dunn

Myths of origin abound in every religious tradition known to humankind. From time immemorial humans have been fascinated and intrigued by the world we inhabit, and how it came to be in the first place. This, however, is a human preoccupation. We feel more in control when we can point to a beginning and an end point. We get a sense of how things started and how they are likely to end. Such terminal points are human abstractions of practical value, which we have long assumed are capable of describing reality as it is. But is reality as simple as that?

Classical science also postulates a beginning and an end: from the big bang until the big crunch. But not quantum physics, nor the evolutionary cosmology of our time. Increasingly today, we view creation as an unfolding process, without beginning or end. It is the process that matters, not the beginning or end points. In terms of our perceptions and understandings, this changes everything, including our theological reference points in relation to God and creation.

Although myths of origin proliferate in the various mythologies of humankind, the Judeo-Christian narrative has influenced scientific rationality on a global scale. Faith in the all-powerful patriarchal God before whom nothing existed—creation ex nihilo—is insinuated in every domain of modern life, including economics and politics as well as science and religion. The postcolonial ideology had long enjoyed metaphysical superiority, until the emergence of a new evolutionary narrative in the twentieth century. Central to that narrative was the discovery of quantum theory, frequently misnamed as *quantum mechanics*.

"Once we step through the portal into a quantum universe," writes Miriam Therese Winter, "we enter into a more whimsical world where the unpredictable is certain, the uncertain is predictable, and the only constant is change" (2009, 8). And it is not merely a new way of doing science, but a paradoxical process with ancient spiritual foundations.

> Practically all the unexpected concepts that quantum physics are using to describe the world were invented by spiritual teachers thousands of years ago. The quantum numbers, the concept of potentiality, the principle of wholeness, the importance of waves as the source of the manifested world—all of these ideas have historically spiritual roots. (Schafer 2013, 21)

The theological horizon we are now beginning to unravel is multidisciplinary in nature, with particular attention to the integration of quantum science and mystical spirituality. And the horizon within which the integration takes place is none other than the cosmic creation at large. For physicist Lothar Schafer, the purpose of the universe "is to take the structure of consciousness to ever increasing levels of integration" (2013, 209).[1]

Out of the Depths

The worldview underpinning quantum physics takes us into the depths. It alerts us to other dimensions of how things begin, and what is at stake in the process known as "beginning."

> How did everything begin? This is the first question faced by any creation myth and . . . answering it remains tricky. . . . Each beginning seems to presuppose an earlier beginning. . . . Instead of meeting a single starting point, we encounter an infinity of them, each of which poses the same problem. . . . There are no entirely satisfactory solutions to this dilemma. What we have to find is not a solution but some way of dealing with the mystery. . . . And we have to do so using words. The words we reach for, from God to gravity, are inadequate to the task. So we have to use language poetically or symbolically; and such language, whether used by a scientist, a poet, or a shaman, can easily be misunderstood. (Christian 2004, 17–18)

"What we have to find is not a solution but some way of dealing with the mystery." These words of David Christian situate the challenge facing us in the present chapter, and the theological reframing of the entire book. The mystery that is creation does not begin merely with the Father God bringing something out of nothing (ex

---

[1] I leave it to the reader to become more versed in the intricate details of quantum physics. Several insights from this field are integrated into the chapters of this book, always exploring the deeper integration between science and spirituality. I have found the following authors to be particularly informed and inspiring in engaging this integration: Paul Levy (2018), Lothar Schafer (2013), and Miriam Therese Winter (2009).

nihilo), a view that is widely held among Christians past and present. The originating mystery is a great deal more subtle and complex.

The original creation is not merely a one-off action of the Creator God, but an unfolding process without beginning or end. For indigenous peoples around the world, Spirit denotes the primordial creative energy that births everything into existence, humans included. This foundational life force is transpersonal, and not merely personal. According to Genesis 1:1–2, it is the foundational, original life force, arising from *ex profundis* (rather than ex nihilo), without beginning or end. It is the divine wellspring of all creativity in whose name everything is declared to be good. And the goodness complexifies according to a creative imperative (a divine eroticism), forever impregnating and sustaining universal life in its multiple diverse expressions.[2]

The notion of "creation out of nothing" is used to emphasize God's ontological being above and beyond all created forms, and has been criticized by Whitney Bauman (2005; 2014) and others as supporting a logic of domination, with deleterious effects not merely for humans but for all forms of organic life. The alternative account of creation, equally based on exegetical scholarship, is *creatio ex profundis* (Keller 2003, 155ff.). As the name implies, creation arises from out of the boundless and expanding depths of the chaos-cosmos rather than being zapped into being from nothing. "The beginning" does not mark a single absolute origin but a "beginning-in-process" that is both "unoriginated and endless." According to Wes Howard-Brook (2010, 51) we are dealing with primeval rather than with historical time. And the creative agent at work is none other than the Spirit who hovers over the waters.

---

[2] For several years now, scientists have also been asking: What was there before the big bang? (see the bibliography in the following webpage: https://science.howstuffworks.com/dictionary/astronomy-terms/before-big-bang1.htm). The very fact that the question keeps arising suggests an issue waiting to be addressed. Here I offer an interdisciplinary integration in which theology provides the catalyst for deeper meaning.

Process theologian Ronald Faber, following the pioneering work of Alfred North Whitehead, suggests that we should understand the story of creation aesthetically rather than causally, with God as the poet of the world erotically luring creation toward self-creativity (Faber 2004, 298). This God is not the one who orders the universe into a fixed structure but rather the luring Spirit who "arranges creation as an adventure, placing it squarely into openness, accompanying it as open wholeness, and keeping its wholeness open. . . . She is instead the Eros that even in her immanence is always transcendent, the Eros in which 'order' is actually an abstraction to which no real significance or meaning can be attributed beyond concrete, living, processual intensity and harmony" (Faber 2004, 118, 229).

The Spirit of God being described here defies all the metaphysical boundaries of conventional pneumatology, exhibiting instead several of the key features of the indigenous notion of the Great Spirit (which I describe at length in O'Murchu 2011). According to Leonardo Boff, "The concept of spirit invites us to see God as a process, as becoming, as the energy that upholds the universe, humanity, and every person. This God is action rather than immutable substance" (2015, 47). In rather esoteric/mystical language, Faber (2004, 287) describes this Spirit of foundational creativity:

> It is in the ecological embedding and wholeness that the "spiritual" aspect of the spirit resides This spirit acquires concreteness, however, not through reason, consciousness, or the freedom of decision . . . but through its preconscious spontaneity and unconscious feeling, its inclination towards intensity and its ecstatic causality, its mutual interpenetration of mentality and corporeality, potentiality and actuality, subjectivity and objectivity, subjective inwardness and rigorous self-surpassing—and all of these things within a specific ecological intertwinement.[3]

---

[3] Similar sentiments are expressed by theologian Leonardo Boff in

The Spirit in Genesis

In light of all the above, the creativity embedded in the open-ing chapters of the book of Genesis needs to be reclaimed, rehabil-itated, and articulated afresh. The spirituality of indigenous tribal peoples, specifically their faith in the Great Spirit, provides an important contemporary aperture into our ancient spirit-inspired creativity, a primordial calling into being more foundational than the "manufacturing" role of the Father/Creator.

In the Hebrew Scriptures (Old Testament), the word *b'reshit* translates as *beginning*, rendering Genesis 1:1 as follows: "In the beginning of God's preparing the heavens and the earth." Other translations are possible and today may be considered more appropriate:

- "In the beginning when God created the heavens and the earth"
- "When God began creating the heavens and the earth"
- "In the beginning of God's creating"

And consider this translation from the original Hebrew: "At the beginning of God's creating of the heavens and the earth, when the earth was wild and waste (*tohu va-vohu*), darkness over the face of the ocean, breath of God hovering over the face of the waters, God said: Let there be light" (Fox 1983, 11).

Beginnings are always taking place, without necessarily marking a definitive newness. Infinite creative possibilities open out from the formless, undifferentiated, and bottomless abyss of primordial chaos (similar to the modern scientific notion of the

---

this inspiring quote: "Everything having to do with the force of fascina-tion, attraction, and union, with the solidarity that includes all, with the forgiveness that reconciles, with the communion that bonds and recon-nects all, with creative fantasy, innovation, invention, creation, extrapo-lation, transcendence, ecstasy, newness, complexity, order, beauty, and with the most varied forms of life, has to do with the Spirit" (2013, 34).

multiverse). There is great depth and darkness to life, and it is a fertile darkness, or what quantum physics names as the *creative vacuum* (cf. King 2001; Davidson 2004). The darksome deep is an ambivalent origin, in contrast to a creation under the mechanism of control and mastery that ex nihilo offers. In the beginning is formless, primal chaos, evoking a feminine, tehomic (sea-centered) language and a refutation of divine omnipotence.

According to the book of Genesis, creation happens in the power of the Word. In Hebrew, however, the word is *Dab(h)ar,* used twenty-four hundred times in the Bible. The Hebrew *Dabar* is used in reference to the "Divine Word" and, in an active sense, as a "word-event" or prophetic word. The Dabar of the Lord carries with it the ability to accomplish what it is sent to do. It also denotes dynamism, filled with a power that is felt by those who receive it, but that is present independently of such reception. Steven R. Service (2015, 59ff.) provides a detailed analysis of how *Dabar* is used in the Hebrew Scriptures, noting that, "Encounter with the Dabar implied impartation of the Spirit" (2015, 74n117). In different books of the Hebrew Scriptures—for example, Psalms, Proverbs, and Jeremiah—the creation is expressly declared to be the work of Wisdom—for which *Dabar* (the Word-as-action) is frequently used. And the holy Dabar is uniquely manifested in the unfolding of creation: the heavens declare the glory of God as the world manifests or reveals the Holy One to our experience.

Memra is Aramaic for "word," which in the Greek is *Logos.* The concept of the *Memra* is derived from Psalm 33:6: "By the word of the Lord were the heavens made; and all the host of them by the breath of his mouth." As early as the first century CE, interpretations (or paraphrases) of religious passages known as Targums began to be written down in Aramaic for Jews who no longer spoke Hebrew. In the Targums, the Jews used the Aramaic word *Memra,* meaning "word," as a personal manifestation of the presence of God.

The Hebrew *Memra,* the Aramaic *Dabar,* the Greek *Logos* (divine rational principle), and the Greek *Rhema* (utterance or things said) all communicate the *Shekenai* or presence of God as a dynamic, empowering, creative life force, identified primarily with that divine source we call the Holy Spirit of God (cf. Service 2015, 46, 74, 99, 178–79, 458, 532). The central issue at stake here—highlighted throughout Service's seminal work—is that Greek rationality (captured in the concept of the *Logos* as rational principle) seriously undermines the creative dynamism inherent in the ancient Hebrew/Aramaic use of the Word. The Greek episte-mological principle of noncontradiction (see Service 2015, 35–46) leaves us with a conceptual and linguistic repertoire unable to grasp the creative, dynamic empowerment communicated in the ancient notions of the *Memra/Dabar* in the Hebrew Scriptures. The foundational empowering relationality of the ancient wisdom was subverted amid the Greek desire for logic and rationality.

For Christians generally, Genesis is about the downfall of humanity, with the woman, Eve, being the primary culprit. Christians seem to easily forget that the narrative begins with the repeated declaration that all in creation is good. However, the storyline quickly moves from divine benevolence to human pre-cariousness. Adam and Eve collude in betraying an original idyllic wholeness, and thereafter disaster and violence explode through-out the entire plot. The Father-Creator God seems to be struggling to manage the violent outpouring, and the creative Spirit is seriously subverted.

Thus far, we are encountering a very different understanding of God compared to the definitive Father-like divine ruler, before whom nothing exists. We are engaged with the "letting-be" God, a Spirit force who loosens up, catalyzes, liberates, and empowers the many breakthroughs that constitute our universal becoming. In the beginning was the Spirit, the energetic life force irrupting from the depths of *ex profundis*. Scientists and theologians have both long suspected the existence of a transcendent, transmaterial life force. "Everyone who is seriously involved in the pursuit of science," asserted the great Albert Einstein, "becomes convinced that a spirit is manifest in the laws of the universe" (quoted in

Levy 2018, 49). The physicist Hans-Peter Dürr (2010, 44) concurs: "As a physicist, I have spent fifty years—my entire life as a researcher—to ask, what is it that hides behind the material. And the result is simple: there is no matter! . . . Basically, there is only spirit." Miriam Therese Winter provides a cryptic and inspiring overview:

> The presence and power of spirit-charged energy will not be constrained by rationality, no matter how hard institutions try to limit it by laws. That which is elusive and ephemeral and eternal cannot be contained, cannot be controlled. God's free-flowing spirit liberates and will not be bound. Spirit is at the heart of all that is, was, and will be, and is in some way one with our own being and becoming. (2009, 76)

Theologian Philip Clayton understands the Holy Spirit as an emergent life force of cosmic significance, and he adopts the notion of *panentheism* to describe the immanent presence of the Spirit throughout the evolving process of creation (2008, 88ff., 133ff.). His central insight is encapsulated in these words:

> The Spirit who emerges corresponds to the Spirit who was present from the beginning, and this Spirit's actions—both its initial creation and its continual lure—help bring about the world and its inhabitants as we know them. In so far as this emergent theology remains panentheistic, it holds that the physical world was already permeated by, and contained within, the Spirit of God long before cosmic evolution gave rise to life and mind. Gone, in this view, are the Spirit-body dualities and those claims for immutability that stem from the world of Greek metaphysics, which once served as the philosophical authority for theology's fundamental categories. (Clayton 2008, 111)

And not merely "theology's fundamental categories," but our very understanding of the notion of God! The linear hierarchical structure of Father, Son, and Holy Spirit, buttressed and dogmatized on the basis of classical Greek metaphysics, has outlived its usefulness and is no longer sustainable within a world ever more amenable to an evolutionary understanding. This foundational role of the Holy Spirit can be discerned on the basis of two of the dynamic forces that both modern science and cosmology understand as foundational to everything in creation, namely *emptiness* and *energy*.

Spirit and the Creative Vacuum

On the vast cosmic scale, emptiness dominates the scene. The as-yet undiscovered dark matter will not fill up the creative emptiness so essential to evolutionary creativity. The vacuum is a sea of fluctuations of tremendous electrical field activity described in modern physics as the zero-point energy. The zero-point energy intimately interacts with everything, from the elementary particles constituting all of matter to the essence of our minds and consciousness. Zero-point energy is the lowest possible level known to science and studied mainly within the sphere of quantum mechanics. Zero-point energy is sometimes used as a synonym for the contents of the vacuum, an amount of energy associated with the vacuum of empty space. When the term is used in this way, it is often referred to as the *quantum vacuum zero-point energy*, otherwise known as the *Higgs field* after the British physicist who discovered it, Peter Higgs (more in László 1998, 180ff.).[4]

---

[4] The Higgs boson created a media frenzy on December 13, 2011, when scientists at the scientific collider at CERN, Geneva, announced that they had detected in the collider debris traces of what looked like the Higgs boson particle. The Higgs field gives mass to particles through a process known as the Higgs mechanism. It is the missing elusive aspect of what scientists call the standard model of particle physics. Reporting this breakthrough, it is noteworthy that heavy emphasis rests on the materiality or physical dimensions (e.g., mass) of particles (atoms)—a

The Higgs field contains a staggering density of energy. The late John Wheeler suggested a measurement of $10^{94}g/cm^3$, amounting to more than all the matter in the known universe. A group of Russian scientists (details in László 1998, 232), exploring the nature and function of the vacuum, postulate the existence of torsion waves, information carriers impacting upon all objects in the universe—from particles to galaxies to the neurons in our brains—with a movement in the rate of 10^9 C, one billion times the speed of light.

These minute spinning structures travel through the vacuum, and they interact with each other. When two or more of these torsion waves meet, they form an interference pattern that integrates the strands of information on the particles that created them. In this way the vacuum records and carries information on atoms, molecules, macromolecules, cells, organisms, and even populations. There is no evident limit to the information that the interfering vacuum torsion waves can conserve and convey. They can, in fact, carry information on the state of the entire universe.

Ervin László (2004) describes the vacuum as an interconnecting Akashic field, with a potential for cosmic interrelatedness far beyond the descriptive potential of either formal science or religion. In Hinduism, *Akasha* refers to the basis and essence of all things in the material world—the smallest material element created from the astral domain. As an underlying field of influence, it is the seedbed of all potentiality, forever eager to explode into

---

crucial part of the machinery of the subatomic world, according to Dr. Stephen Barr of Oxford University (UK). Yet we know that over 99 percent of the atom is empty space, which may in fact be far more crucial to our understanding of the subatomic world than materiality or physicality, as suggested by Pim van Lommel (2010, 283ff.). Identifying the Higgs Boson may be significant for mainline scientific progress, but there is a deeper and more pervasive truth to the subatomic world, which the media excitement overlooks and the reporting fails to acknowledge.

form. Within this all-embracing field force, consciousness seems to play a crucial role, a cosmic transcendent force that quantum theory dances around without yet having the wherewithal to name its pregnant potential. Of all the scholars I have consulted on this daring new horizon (of consciousness), I find the reflections of Dutch cardiologist-cum-scientist Pim van Lommel (2010) to be most persuasive and compelling. Consciousness may well be the most responsible and creative way to the connective tissue of universal life, reminiscent of the wisdom and intelligence we associate with that underlying divine empowerment that theology calls the Holy Spirit of God.

The observations above can help us to appreciate the counterintuitive truth that the vacuum state, or the quantum vacuum, is anything but "empty." It thrives on overload, but at an elusive, and even mysterious, level still being investigated by modern science. According to quantum mechanics, the vacuum state is not truly empty but instead contains fleeting electromagnetic waves and particles that continually pop into and out of existence. Brian Swimme provides a vivid illustration in his reflections on the "cupped hands":

> Cup your hands together and imagine what you are holding. First in quantum terms would be the molecules of air, the molecules of nitrogen, oxygen, carbon dioxide, and other trace gases. There would be many more than a billion trillion. If we imagine removing every one of these atoms, we would be left holding extremely small particles such as neutrinos from the sun. In addition, there would be radiation energy in the form of invisible light, such as photons from the original flaring forth of the universe. In other words, to get down to nothingness we would have to remove not only all the subatomic particles; we would also have to remove each and every one of these invisible particles of light.

But now imagine we have somehow done this, so
that in your cupped hands there are no molecules left,
and no particles, and no photons of light. All matter and
radiation have been removed. No things would be left,
no objects, no stuff, no items that could be counted or
measured. What would remain would be what we modern peoples refer to as the "vacuum" or "emptiness" or
"pure space."

Now for the news: careful investigation of this vacuum by quantum physicists reveals the strange appearance of elementary particles in this emptiness. Even where
there are no atoms, and no elementary particles, and no
protons, and no photons, suddenly elementary particles
will emerge. The particles simply foam into existence. . . .
The particles emerge from the "vacuum." They do not
sneak in from some hiding place when we are not looking. Nor are they bits of light energy that have transformed into protons. These elementary particles crop up
out of the vacuum, itself—this is the simple and awe-
some discovery. I am asking you to contemplate a universe where, somehow, being itself arises out of a field of
"fecund emptiness." (1996, 92–93)

The basic idea is this: The vacuum, or nothing-with-special-
dimensions, is actually a real energy field or state of subtle material substance, out of which all perceivable matter is formed and
within which are found, in finer levels of manifestation, the energy
fields from which arise even our personal thoughts, feelings, and
instincts.

Not surprisingly we encounter a similar truth in the realm
of the really small, the world of atoms and cells that is invisible
to the human eye. An atom consists of a tiny nucleus (a pro-
ton) surrounded by over 99 percent empty space. Although the
nucleus of a hydrogen atom consists of three quarks, they need to

be envisaged as "points" or, according to string theory, vibrations of energy. At the atomic level, solidity plays a minor role.

We find a similar case with a molecule, the basic unit of chemical interaction in all living systems. A molecule is defined as an electrically neutral group of at least two atoms in a definite arrangement, held together by very strong chemical bonds. Cells, the basic units in biology, comprise interactive molecules. However, the wisdom and power of the cell are captured more succinctly in Deepak Chopra's insightful description: "a cell is memory with membrane wrapped round it" (Chopra 1989, 87). Once again, creative emptiness engages the human imagination, and I suppose it takes something akin to the "pneumatological imagination" (Yong 2005, 28) to truly engage this fertile emptiness.

All Is Energy

The second key metaphor in our attempt to understand the originating Spirit is that of energy. In the words of theologian Peter Hodgson,

> Spirit is an immaterial vitality that enlivens and shapes material creation. It is the *energeia* that infuses all that is. . . . It is the relationality that holds things together even as it keeps them distinct. It is a desire or eros at once intellectual and sensuous. . . . Spirit is nothing without relations; it is precisely relationality, the moving air that permeates and enlivens things, the open space across which the wind of Spirit blows. (1994, 280, 284)

In classical physics we describe energy in terms of its usefulness for driving machines (including the big machine of the universe itself) and for sustaining our capacity to engage with the challenges of daily life. In this understanding energy has a materially quantifiable character. As understood by quantum physics,

however, energy carries a different meaning as a wavelike potentiality, creating and sustaining everything that exists.

Subatomic particles are seen by modern physics more as
smears of existential probability with wavelike and vibrational
properties, rather than as solid blobs resembling billiard balls.
"Very clearly," writes John Davidson, "the particles are coming
out of 'nothing,' out of the vacuum. There is nowhere else for
them to arise. So 'nothing' must be 'something.' . . . From our
understanding of the vacuum matrix we can see how all manifestation is a pattern, a dance, an affect given specific 'reality,'
and linked to our consciousness through our sensory perception"
(2004, 30, 43).

Instead of envisaging the elements of creation as minute entities
called particles, *string theory* suggests that creation is made up of
vibrations of energy, similar to the resonances obtained when playing a musical instrument such as a guitar (more in Green 2000).
Creation is constituted by musiclike sound, manifesting as strings.
These strings are so small that even when looked at very closely
they may resemble points. Each basic particle is created by the
strings vibrating in different patterns. What makes this theory particularly attractive to scientists is that gravitons (the ingredients of
gravity) can also be mathematically described, a feat not possible
in other approaches. What makes the theory difficult to substantiate scientifically is the fact that it requires *ten* dimensions, and not
merely the standard *four* (three spatial factors and one of time), the
other *six* being compacted and therefore not easily analyzed.

Excitement is scarcely containable on this esoteric subject.
To date, scientists have come up with six different string theories (supergravity being the sixth—requiring an eleven-dimen-
sional configuration). Best known is M-theory, devised in 1995
by American physicist Edward Witten. This theory combines
five different string theories (along with a previously abandoned attempt to unify general relativity and quantum mechanics called 11D-Supergravity) into one theory. In M-theory, we

meet the notion of the *brane,* related to the word *membrane.* This terminology is used to unravel the deeper secrets within the mathematics in which the extra space dimensions in a membrane are considered to consist of two branes. A string is called a one-brane, and a point is called a zero-brane. M-theory states that strings of energy could grow into larger membranes or branes even up to the size of the universe.

What does it all mean? Among other things it highlights that mystical pursuit that never ceases to drive the human spirit. Two observations are pertinent here, which are explored further throughout this book: (1) We already know about the innate curiosity of the human mind; I want to further suggest that it is essentially *spiritual* in nature, and has been awakened in each of us by that inner life force we call the Great Spirit (or Holy Spirit in the Christian religion); (2) more controversially, we seek deeper understanding of the creation we inhabit because the universe itself is inhabited by an inexhaustible life force that awakens our curiosity in the first place, and forever lures us to look deeply within, for therein are the depths that assure us that the mystery we inhabit is fundamentally sacred and benign.

Meaning from Within

Scientists like clarity, precision, and rigorous objectivity. As far as they are concerned, dealing with imponderables is best left to philosophers or others who dabble in esoteric matters. Nonetheless, we do encounter great thinkers whose human grounding in mystery still remains intact. We get valuable glimpses from the journals, letters, and private notes of the great Albert Einstein. And in relation to the quantum vacuum, here is a gem from renowned German physicist Max Planck (allegedly from a lecture he gave in Florence, Italy, in 1944):

> As a man who has devoted his whole life to the most clear-headed science, the study of matter, I can tell you, as

a result of my research about the atoms, this much: There
is no matter as such. All matter originates and exists only
by virtue of a force which brings the particles of an atom
to vibration and holds the most minute solar system of
the atom together. . . . We must assume behind this force
that existence of a conscious and intelligent Mind. This
Mind is the matrix of all matter.

"No matter as such"! Only the creative emptiness! And the
creativity is sustained by some kind of consciousness, intelligence,
or Mind: dare we name it *Spirit-Power*? Our reflections on the
nature and workings of the creative vacuum lead to a number of
significant insights:

- There exists in the entire creation a kind of "within-ness"
  that cannot be quantified or measured and seems to defy
  all attempts at human analysis or explanation. Mysterious, yet inescapably real.
- The meaning of creation and its complex functioning comes
  first and foremost from within, not from without (in terms
  of human comprehension or objective verification).
- The force-from-within is restless, mobile, and pregnant
  with possibility for external expression at a whole range
  of levels, including material form.
- The sense of generativity seems unassailable—and as
  modern physics suggests, infinite (cf. László 2004, 30),
  noting that the infinity in question is not about life hereafter, nor a particular characteristic of the divine, but an
  enduring quality of our open-ended universe.
- There seems to be a sense of direction to what emanates
  from the creative vacuum, what science refers to as the
  arrow of time—not to be confused with the notion of
  intelligent design.[5] The direction seems to be toward

---

[5] Intelligent design refers to a scientific research program as well

greater and more abundant creativity, complexity, and enrichment—with a great deal of chaos and experiment included.

- The force from within begets structure (e.g., particles, atoms, and the material forms of creation), but on closer examination, it first engenders a capacity for relating (relationships), without which structure is unlikely to evolve.

- Max Planck postulates a Mind behind (or within) the whole process; Van Lommel (2010) and Paul Levy (2018) call it *consciousness*; while physicist Jude Currivan describes it as "intelligible in-formation, exquisitely balanced, incredibly co-creative, staggeringly powerful, and yet fundamentally simple" (2017, 181). I name it as Great Spirit (what the Christian religion calls Holy Spirit). It is fundamentally transpersonal, not personal or impersonal, a distinction clarified later in this book.

---

as to a community of scientists, philosophers, and other scholars who seek evidence of design in nature. The theory of intelligent design (ID) holds that certain features of the universe and of living things are best explained by an intelligent cause, not an undirected process such as natural selection. ID theory claims that the intelligent causes are necessary to explain the complex, information-rich structures of biology and that these causes are empirically detectable. Certain biological features defy the standard Darwinian random-chance explanation, because those promoting an ID stance claim that they have been designed by a divine, intelligent power. The vast majority of intelligent design theorists are theists. They see the appearance of design that pervades the biological world as evidence for the existence of God. However, the intelligent design theory is not biblical creationism. There is an important distinction between the two positions. Biblical creationists begin with a conclusion that the biblical account of creation is reliable and correct, that life on Earth was designed by an intelligent agent—God. They then look for evidence from the natural realm to support this conclusion. For a valuable overview and critique, see Haught (2003, 85ff.).

Spirit Will Not Be Bound!

That the universe came into being ex nihilo (from nothing), whether via a big bang, or some inflationary expansion, is still the favored theory of many scientists. However, the jury is still out, and the longer it stays out, the more compelling and credible are the words of John Davidson (2004, 131), which I'd like to use as a focus for collecting the main insights of this chapter:

> The secret of the subatomic world must lie in the mystic construction of the creation from within-out, a holographically woven tapestry of polarity, pattern and relationship, reflected in the nature of its inward structure and dimensionality.

Consequently, it is not so much about a creation from nothing (ex nihilo) as rather an emergence from profound depths, which Catherine Keller named *ex profundis* (see also Robinette 2011, esp. 525–32; Lee 2014, 202–5). Deep down is an intelligence, a source of meaning and possibility that defies all our rational theories, and indeed all our theological dogmas as well. It is difficult to avoid the conclusion that this is the Great Spirit so long cherished by the world's indigenous peoples, ancient and modern alike.

We have not disposed of the notion of the Trinity, but we are certainly in the process of reframing it substantially. That essential relatedness cannot be captured by dogma, whether religious or scientific. Thankfully it eludes all our attempts at finality! Beyond the human boundaries of origins and endings, there moves an energetic spirit, uncreated and itself without beginning or end. Surely, this is where our theological reconstruction has to begin.

By honoring that spirit-inspired imperative, we protect both God and ourselves from the idolatry that has bedeviled human civilization for the past few thousand years. We allow God to be God, in terms more congruent to how we view God at work in creation, and not in accordance with philosophical tenets of whatever source.

And this process is neither pantheism nor panentheism. Rather it is an attempt at honoring divine action at work, first and foremost in the universal process of creation, long before humans ever evolved or before religious systems came into being. In that evolving, dynamic, and paradoxical process we discern revelatory intent; we see God at work, and the divine bestowal of love and life, of creativity and evolution.

For that creative God there was no such thing as an idyllic past that religion forever tries to recapture and reclaim. Evolution is always open and free, and for most of the time highly paradoxical.[6] If there is no idyllic past, neither can there be a fall from grace, an issue we address in a later chapter. Waiting for redemption is a waste of precious time and sacred energy. Instead, we are meant to be participators in a participatory universe, forever co-birthing with spirit-infused energy endowing and gracing every aspect of our lives. That invitation to new birthing is the topic of our next chapter.

---

[6] And evolution is always operating through the paradoxical process of creation-cum-destruction or the cyclic pattern of birth-death-rebirth. I review this topic in several previous works, notably O'Murchu (2002; 2011; 2017).

7

Creation as Embodied Birthing

A society that believes that the body is somehow diseased, painful, sinful, or wrong . . . is going to create social institutions out of those body-denying attitudes that wreak destruction not only on human, plant, and other creaturely bodies but on the body of the Earth herself.

Paula Gunn Allen

God's Spirit breathes the world into being, dwells in all things, quickens love into flame, inspires the prophets, and renews the face of the earth.

Elizabeth Johnson

The original depths—Catherine Keller's *ex profundis*—are endowed with an emergent orientation, with becoming and flourishing inscribed in its dynamic flow. It sounds like creation could do no other than to flourish, blossom forth, and grow in complexity. This insight also poses new questions for the notion of an original divine Creator: Do we need such a postulate? Is there not already enough evidence in the meaning-laden process of evolution itself (a question we address in the next chapter)? We find that the notion of creation as embodied birthing may indeed be more compelling and persuasive than our elaborate dogmas of an outstanding patriarchal male, often employed to justify and validate the patriarchal will to domination and control.

Two key insights engage us in the present chapter: (1) Spirit needs body in order to manifest and structure its energizing presence, and (2) the notion of God as creator carries more evolutionary meaning when we envisage God as a Great Birther rather than the male patriarchal creator who operates ex nihilo.

The Body and Embodiment

Our modern world is bedeviled with a very reductionistic understanding of the body, and religion has been a major influence in this restricted perception. Upon hearing the word "body," most people immediately assume that we are alluding to the human body, widely regarded as the most evolutionarily advanced expression of embodiment in the universe. That superior status is largely due to Aristotle, for whom the human body is ensouled to a degree that exalts its significance above all other forms of embodiment. And by all other forms, most people assume those deemed to be inferior to the human, specifically the animals.

Throughout the latter half of the twentieth century, both the social and physical sciences surfaced a very different understanding of the body. The universe itself came to be regarded as the foundational form of embodiment from which all other organisms, including human beings, derive their embodied integrity. Obviously, this is not the mechanistic worldview to which classical science still clings, but rather the more organic view upheld by quantum physics. Herein, the cosmos and all other organisms have evolved from the creative vacuum, emergent outcomes of its pregnant energy. The outcome is not so much that of *beings* (in the metaphysical sense) but rather *becomings*, events in process and not merely physical or biological entities.

Several philosophers have embraced and articulated afresh the ensuing challenge. David Abram (1996; 2010), relying mainly on the anthropology of Maurice Merleau-Ponty (1908–1961), provides a valuable overview of this new approach:

> We humans are corporeally related, by direct and indirect webs of evolutionary affiliation, to *every* other organism that we encounter. Moreover, it is not only other animals, plants, and simpler organisms that have contributed, during the course of evolution, to the unique character of the human creature, but also the fluid ocean, and the many rocks that compose the soils, and the way the mountains gather clouds above the high ridges. These planetary structures are not extrinsic to human life—*they are not arbitrary or random aspects of a world we just happen to inhabit*. Rather they are the constitutive powers that summoned us into existence, and hence are the secret allies, the totemic guides, of all our actions. They are as much within us as they are around us; they compose the wider, deeper life of which our bodies are a part. (Abram 2010, 77–78)

Traditionally, all that is extrinsic to the physical body we attribute to the spiritual power of the soul, at one time understood as the life force inserted into the biological stuff by some type of divine intervention. Here we detect the haunting influence of dualistic splitting between the sacred and the secular. Today, the perennial challenge is to understand and befriend the foundational sacredness of all reality. The concept of soul is no longer useful or relevant; *Spirit* is the phenomenon with which we need to engage.

All creation is in-spirited, as adumbrated by several contemporary theologians (e.g., Mark Wallace, Denis Edwards, Leonardo Boff, John Haughey, Elizabeth Johnson, and Sallie McFague). As outlined in the last chapter, this is the creative enduring energy, without beginning or end. This is the life force, from which all life-forms are begotten and evolve—from the vast universe (multiverse) to the subatomic particles, and from the foundational bacteria to human organisms. In scientific terms this is the underlying in-formation that intelligently and creatively informs all life (more in Currivan 2017). The Spirit is the mighty originating and sustaining catalyst, more primordial than the traditional father-creator, whose power to create is itself conferred by the Great Spirit. Yet, despite this creative elegance, it appears that the creativity of the Spirit requires bodies to mediate and facilitate this creative potential. On its own, it seems that the Spirit can achieve little. It is when the Spirit is poured out on all flesh (Acts 2:17) that new life, generativity, and hope unfold—on a global scale. "Whatever transcendence is ascribed to Spirit," writes Margaret A. Farley (2006, 130), "must also be ascribed to body—for they are intimately one."

This oneness in the flesh takes on additional significance when we note the distinction between the Hebrew word for flesh, *basar*, and the Greek term used by St. Paul, *sarx*. While the latter denotes alienation from God through sinful tendencies and behavior, *basar* "takes its primary meaning from the material substance of which earthly creatures are made. . . . It can refer to a human person as a psychosomatic individual, to kinfolk or relatives (my flesh and blood), or to all humankind. Beyond humans it can refer to animals, to meat for eating or sacrificing, and very broadly to all living things" (Johnson 2018, 162).[1]

The creative Spirit is not merely about purifying the flesh, or worse still, desiring its final destruction and elimination. On the contrary, it is in and through the flesh (*basar*) that the Spirit inspires and empowers, activates creativity, and illuminates the mystery within which we live, move, and have our being. The old-

---

[1] Johnson also acknowledges that "While the term can sometimes be used to mean hostility to God, most often in scripture it refers not to sin but to finitude, to being limited and mortal, which in itself is not sinful" (2018, 162).

est known human source of that integral, cosmic, transpersonal understanding seems to be that of the world's indigenous peoples and their understanding of God as Great Spirit, a topic I explore at length in a previous work (O'Murchu 2011), and review briefly in the last chapter of this book.

Creative Birthing

So foundational are new life and its infinite possibilities, one begins to understand why the creative function of the divine assumed such an exalted status. However, the paternalistic, patriarchal description is no longer appropriate as it undermines the empowering creativity that belongs primordially to the Great Spirit. Another metaphorical naming serves us much better, namely, the notion of God as the Great Birther. Empowered by the creative Spirit, the divine life force in the world forever gives birth—to stars and galaxies, planets and bacteria, flowers and humans.

Mystics of all faith traditions have long relished this birthing metaphor. Often cited is the fanciful strophe of Meister Eckhart: "What does God do all day long? God gives birth. From all eternity God lies on a maternity bed giving birth."[2] Had Christianity adopted that metaphor, rather than the prevailing ones of God as King, Ruler, Judge, and so on, we would have an entirely different theology today, one far more congruent with the theological awakening of the twenty-first century.

Birthing, of course, as a much more feminine metaphor, has strong female and maternal significance—and it is unmistakably corporeal. The fact that the mother carries the child in her womb for nine months evidences before all else how central embodiment is to the birthing of new life. While the creation ex nihilo (creation out of nothing) denotes a God above and outside embodied processes of creation at large, the metaphor of a birthing God

---

[2] Matthew Fox, *Meditations with Meister Eckhart* (Santa Fe, NM: Bear and Co., 1982), 88.

includes everything that is sensuous, visceral, erotic, and generative. This image is far more congruent with the Christian notion of Immanuel, a God who abides deeply, lovingly, and unconditionally in the midst of every pregnant, and birthing, breakthrough.

Such birthing also resonates with the ever new and fresh awakenings that sustain the evolutionary process, along with the nurturance necessary to sustain, protect, and promote all that is wholesome, good, and fruitful. While in biological terms birthing is often mediated by an individual, the nurturing aspect tends to be strongly communitarian. "It takes a village to rear a child" is an adage known in several cultures. And as primatologist Sarah Blaffer Hrdy (2009) indicates, such nurturance is not merely indicative of love and care, but also becomes the basis for a psychic imprinting whereby humans—and other organisms—are foundationally programmed for cooperative, communal endeavors.

Beyond the monotheistic preoccupation with the imperial creator, ruling, controlling, and directing from on high, the birthing God belongs to the round, to the formative collaborative circle at the basis of every co-evolutive process. In the words of theologian Peter Hodgson, "God is the light that illumines, the word that discloses, the reason that communicates, the love that cherishes, the freedom that liberates, the revelatoriness that reveals, the being by which beings are." He continues, "God is the event of worldly unconcealment by which new meaning and new possibilities of being are created. . . . God is neither an entity in the world nor an entity outside it but the revelatory-communicative-emancipatory event-process-power by which the world is" (Hodgson 1994, 132).

Here empowerment, rather than patriarchal power, is the crucial dynamic at work. And the emphasis is not on what the creator can achieve on his own, but on the many others—indeed, the entire web of cosmic and planetary life—who are engaged in the collaborative process. Hence, the simple but profound declaration in John 15:15: "I do not call you servants, but friends."

Before we ever even arrive at the Christian story, incarnation is already flourishing throughout the entire spectrum of universal planetary life. Incarnation is all about embodiment. The body is the primary organism employed by the Great Birther for the metamorphosis of the Spirit's empowering energy.[3] Bodies—all bodies—are the living revelation of the divine birthing, operative throughout creation since the dawn of time.

Bringing Jesus to Birth

Throughout the Christian world the birth of Jesus is marked with a great deal of myth, ritual, and custom. Much of it can be traced to older sources, typically described as pagan or primitive. In fact, the symbolism is quite complex and usually escapes the rational analysis of both the Scripture scholar and the theologian.

The infancy narratives tend to be interpreted literally, thus undermining the rich symbolic and metaphoric texture of the storied event. Precisely because the storytellers (and later writers) are narrating a unique birthing-forth of divine creativity, overstatement is inherent to such communication. And yet the context is embedded in ordinariness, as the extraordinary and the ordinary meet with a quality of integration that rational discourse can never adequately comprehend or describe.

Some of the subtle features of the context of Jesus's birth need to be noted. Following several mythic narratives about origins and beginnings (e.g., the Egyptian, Osiris [Horus]; the Greek, Zeus and Dionysus; the Persian, Mithra; and the Indian, Mitra), Jesus is also deemed to be of remarkable birth, arising from a miraculous divine intervention. Such intervention is typically mediated by heavenly beings, usually angels, and there is a tendency to dualistically split the human and the divine, obviously with the

---

[3] Constrained by the limitations of language, it looks as if I am separating the Birther and the Spirit into totally different roles and functions. Just as we cannot separate the three "persons" of the classical Trinity, neither can we delineate the three in the newly envisaged Trinitarian construct that I am proposing.

divine having prerogative. Both the natural world (e.g., shepherds) and extraordinary human powers (such as kings) are portrayed as subservient to the newly divine imperial-type figure. Typically, such divine intervention is mediated by a male, who already as a child is endowed with magical, superhuman powers. In this process we bypass, and try to subvert, the inherited belief that Mary conceived out of wedlock, and therefore Jesus would have been an illegitimate child (see Schaberg 1987).

What we are encountering here is a rebirth of imperial power. While the Spirit may indeed be the impregnating force, Christianity typically describes its incarnational narrative as God sending his beloved Son. The Spirit is subverted amid the imperial grandeur. Moreover, the embodiment through which the birthing happens is also defective in several ways. With the ensuing rhetoric of Mary's virginity, and a pregnancy resulting from divine intervention rather than earthly human intercourse, disembodiment comes to the fore, with a trail of disastrous consequences for both women and the earth. Jesus is portrayed as an angelic transhuman being, rather than an icon for God's radical immersion in the earthly, human condition.

The infancy narratives of Matthew and Luke still retain some of those grounding features that honor a more authentic, and earthly, context. Unfortunately, the features are often used to uphold Semitic (anti-Jewish) rhetoric: "He came to his own and his own received him not" (Jn 1:11). Even if Jesus was born out of wedlock, such was the quality of Jewish hospitality that it is very likely Jesus would have been born within a Jewish household. Joseph would have ensured this for Mary. And even as an illegitimate child, he would still receive warmth, love, and care on par with every other newborn.

In all probability, Jesus was not born in some mountain cave, nor was he the victim of the "no room in the inn" situation described, for example, in Luke 2:7. In the emergency of the moment Mary may have had to share the lower ground floor, where the animals were usually housed, but regularly used for unexpected guests. Consequently, the presence of animals at the Christmas crib may indeed be highly symbolic. Jesus was birthed into the world amid the ordinariness of daily life and earthly conditions. The divine embodiment is human and earthly to its very core.

Yet the ordinariness is supplemented with the extraordinary, better understood in archetypal terms rather than as the progeny of divine intervention. Mary is described as a virgin—*parthenos* in Greek, but *almah* in the Hebrew background suggested by Matthew's employment of Isaiah 7:14. Had Isaiah wished to speak about a virgin, he would have used the word *betulah,* not *almah.* The word *betulah* appears frequently in the Jewish Scriptures, and is the only word—in both biblical and modern Hebrew—that conveys sexual purity.[4]

In the Gospel account, Mary is declared to be a virgin, which in biological terms means that her hymen has not been penetrated and therefore she has never had sexual intercourse with a man. However, as many commentators point out and as noted above, in describing Mary's virginity, we encounter a confusing picture between the Greek *parthenos* and the Hebrew *almah* (see Is 7:14). The latter has nothing to do with biological virginity; rather, it denotes a young woman of marriageable age, and of outstanding character. Theologian Elizabeth Johnson affirms a more ancient and archetypal meaning for virginity: "To be a virgin is to be one in yourself, free, independent, insubordinated, unexploited, a woman never subdued" (2003, 239).

Scholars agree that *almah* refers to a woman of childbearing age without implying virginity. Archetypally, however, the word carries a wider, more complex significance. The virgin archetype

---

[4] In fact, although Isaiah used the Hebrew word *almah* only once (7:14), the prophet uses this word *virgin (betulah)* five times (23:4; 23:12; 37:22; 47:1; 62:5). Noteworthy, too, is the derivation of *almah* from the Persian Al-Mah, the unmated moon goddess. Another cognate of this term was the Latin *alma,* "living soul of the world," which is essentially identical to the Greek *psyche* and the Sanskrit *shakti.*

has an intense inner focus. She is spiritually orientated and more concerned with the inner world than the outer realm, yet from deep within that inner depth is a resourcefulness capable of birthing forth life at every level of creation, from the vast galaxies to minuscule subatomic particles. For women particularly, the archetype represents a sexualized fertility not to be confined to intimate partnerships, motherhood, or child rearing.[5] The virgin (or *maiden*) represents the power of birthing, enchantment, inception, expansion, the promise of new beginnings, and birth, represented by the waxing moon. In archetypal terms, it is she who gives birth to all creation from galaxies right down to the smallest bacteria.

And the Birthing Continues

Even Jesus had to submit to the process of birthing, in and through a human sexual relationship, whether in or out of wedlock. The nurturance of the newborn infant was facilitated by a range of embodied creatures, archetypally named as Mary, Joseph, angels, shepherds, kings, and a cohort of unnamed Jewish friends and neighbors. And as with all birthing, the heavens rejoiced and so did the earth.

How the birthing continued in the early years of the historical Jesus is completely unknown to us. That he might have been a *teckton* (woodworker), possibly involved in the construction of big cities like Tiberias and Sepphoris, is a distinct possibility, once more grounding him in an embodied relationship with his culture and its environment. His later affiliation with John the Baptist may suggest a spiritual seeker exploring other ways to embody faith and spiritual meaning. And both his eventual parting from

---

[5] Not surprising, therefore, we find among the ancient goddesses the paradoxical reality that they are often unmarried, but this did not mean that they were necessarily asexual. In fact, some of the virgin goddesses expressed their sexuality openly, owning their sexuality proudly and without shame. It was not given away or bartered or owned by their partners; it was wholly and solely within their own dominion.

John's ascetical model and his option for a highly controversial affiliation with prostitutes, tax collectors, and sinners created an embodied form of empowerment that Christianity wrestles with to this day.

St. Paul, despite the complex nature of his teachings and writings, and his apparent expectation of the world ending in his lifetime, continued the birthing and the embodiment of Jesus's empowering mission.[6] He did it through small *ecclesial* groups that were fluid, flexible, and creative. And from these seminal basic ecclesial communities (BECs) evolved the notion of Christians being the body of Christ on earth. Now the birthing—and its continuous embodiment—became our human responsibility, and something in which we have failed rather miserably!

Over the centuries we have been dogged with apocalyptic waiting. "When is God [or Jesus] going to intervene again and rescue us?" we continually ask. We have had no shortage of fear-mongering about death and punishment, along with a final judgment when God returns to bring everything to completion. It is tragic that so many people have been hoodwinked by such crazy rhetoric.

There will be no coming back, no divine judgment, nor an "end of the world"—other than the apocalyptic possibility that we will destroy ourselves as a species. The coming of Jesus in the first place was never about a divine intervention (as we shall see in the next chapter). Rather it was part of an evolutionary imperative of humanity growing into a deeper sense of incarnation. And that new incarnational embodiment is about us (humanity), and not about God or Jesus.

Scripture scholar John Dominic Crossan, in several of his writings, highlights the challenge facing us in these words: "While we are waiting for God's intervention, God is actually waiting

---

[6] This despite the fact that Paul frequently seems to support the patriarchal power that he also contests, in the kind of mimicry frequently noted by postcolonial scholars (more in Stanley 2011).

on our collaboration" (see Crossan 2010, 89–90). God's birth-ing of life, and our call to be co-birthers with our birthing God, has nothing to do with waiting for divine interventions. In his life, Jesus has already left us a strategy for a different quality of engagement, one of collaboration and not of being mere passive recipients forever waiting for a divine rescue.

Along with all the creatures of God's creation we are blessed and energized by the living Spirit of God, God's first and foun-dational giftedness to all beings. In the power of that Spirit we embrace the task of birthing, renewing the face of the earth, for-ever sensitive and responsive to the Spirit's evolutionary impera-tive. As co-birthers with our birthing God, we both receive and give, in the collaborative endeavor that Jesus modeled for us in the Gospel strategy of the kingdom of God (further explored in chapter 9).

Healing the Wounded Body

Over the centuries, theology has not dealt well with the embodied birthing that characterizes the creative process at every level of God's creation. Because of this neglect we are left with a range of embodied perversions that cry out for healing and wholeness. All over the planet, in poor and rich countries alike, the human body is in pain, overtly because of violence, warfare, poverty, and oppression. In several such cases, the suf-fering of the human body is actually a consequence of the tor-tured earth body. When we desecrate creation's body, we harm ourselves as well. Both embodied expressions are intimately con-nected at all times.

For those on our planet exposed to the violence of war, oppression, and patriarchal domination, humans can reach remarkable levels of pain tolerance. To survive they know they have to endure, and will endure often to extenuating lengths. For those among us who live in cultures of relative peace and prosper-ity the pain is suppressed (and often repressed) in ways that can leave behind a legacy of even deeper alienation. Two pertinent examples are the cult of the beautiful body and the use of plastic surgery for body enhancement.

In 1979, Christopher Lasch, a historian at the University of Rochester, published what became a top seller in the United States, *The Culture of Narcissism*, diagnosing a pathology that seemed to have spread to all corners of American life. In Lasch's definition (drawn from Freud), the narcissist, driven by repressed rage and self-hatred, escapes into a grandiose self-conception, using other people as instruments of gratification even while craving their love and approval. This culture of rising self-absorption (often described as rampant individualism) morphed into several expressions, among them a highly commercialized market for cosmetic makeup and clothing fashions, feeding what seemed like an insatiable hunger for body fulfillment.

A further expression of the same hunger is that of the growing adaptation of plastic surgery for body enhancement. Of the nearly 1.8 million cosmetic surgical procedures performed in the United States in 2017, the top five were as follows:

Breast augmentation (300,378 procedures, up 3 percent from 2016)

Liposuction (246,354 procedures, up 5 percent from 2016)

Nose reshaping (218,924 procedures, down 2 percent from 2016)

Eyelid surgery (209,571 procedures, approximately the same as 2016)

Tummy tuck (129,753 procedures, up 2 percent from 2016)

In the United States alone, in 2018, an estimated 18 million people underwent a cosmetic procedure, for a total bill of $8.6 billion. What is often not reported is the further expenditure of subsequent corrective surgery, highlighted by Pereira, Malone, and Flaherty (2018). Culturally and theologically, one asks: why are millions of people so dissatisfied with their bodies? Even among those who embrace an embodied-centered faith like Christianity, this unease with the body seems to be quite widespread. And how much of our "dis-ease" with the body is a consequence of a species that has become severely disconnected from the earth body in which millions no longer seem to be organically grounded?

While this incestuous preoccupation with the body, and its personal inflation, is extensively noted, and frequently subjected to negative appraisal, a much deeper discernment seems to be necessary. To what extent are we evidencing a reaction to a repression of bodily desire that goes back several centuries, perhaps even a few millennia? In the Christian context, we have inherited a philosophical anthropology, widely adopted culturally and religiously—but upon closer examination, this inheritance has seriously undermined a more wholesome way of being human.

Prior to the Agricultural Revolution (some ten thousand years ago), we humans seem to have lived in a much more embodied and grounded way, close to the earth's organicity, flowing with the natural rhythms of life, intimate with the sensuous, relaxed with sexual pleasure. In Christopher Boehm's *Hierarchy in the Forest: The Evolution of Egalitarian Behavior,* he writes: "This egalitarian approach appears to be universal for foragers who live in small bands that remain nomadic, suggesting considerable antiquity for political egalitarianism" (1999, 69). In Paleolithic times many of our most fundamental values, practices such as ownership and private property, did not exist. There were no chiefs, no bosses, no headmen, and no police. There was no money. Kinship was matriarchal. Monotheism, with its sanctioning of the one supreme patriarchal authority, had not yet evolved.

"Hunter-gatherers almost everywhere are known for being fiercely egalitarian and going to great lengths to downplay competition and forestall ruptures in the social fabric, for reflexively shunning, humiliating, even ostracizing or executing those who behave in stingy, boastful, and antisocial ways," writes primatologist Sarah Blaffer Hrdy (2009, 20). The human capacity for cooperation has been long ignored (and probably suppressed) as a valid field for exploration. In our time, Matt Ridley launched a new wave of investigation in his 1996 publication, *The Origins of Virtue*, to be followed in the opening years of the twenty-first century by a plethora of new works, many of them rigorously scientific. These include Hrdy's 2009 work, *Mothers and Others*; Jeremy Rifkin's acclaimed volume *The Empathic Civilization* (2010), highlighting the co-evolution of empathy and entropy in our time; Frans de Waal's *The Age of Empathy*, which traces our cooperative streak right back to some of our animal and primate ancestors (de Waal 2010); Christopher Boehm's *Moral Origins* (2012), which argues that an ancient form of radical egalitarianism underpins our moral conscience; and Samuel Bowles and Herbert Gintis's *A Cooperative Species* (2013), which provides a scholarly genetic-based analysis of how cooperation and altruistic concern evolved in our species.

Contrary to the harsh moralistic judgments of the monotheistic religions, our hunter-gatherer ancestors maintained levels of personal and interpersonal integration and creativity that would put many of us to shame today. Theirs was a very different anthropology from ours, one in which the human body operated within a much deeper incarnational dignity. Things apparently took a rather negative turn with the emergence of classical Greek philosophy, particularly in the theories of Plato and Aristotle. For both of them, what is critically important is what differentiates the human from all else, and especially from the animals. For the Greeks, this key differentiating factor is the *soul*, which for both Plato and Aristotle becomes the seat of *reason*.

This emphasis on rationality is not merely a human endowment. For Aristotle it is a divine quality: "The human being is the only erect animal because its nature and essence is divine; the function of the most divine is thinking and being intelligent" (*De partibus animalium* IV.10 686a 27–29). In both the *Nichomachean Ethics* and in *De Anima*, part 3, Aristotle writes extensively about human flourishing and the happiness (*eudaimonia*) that ensues. Indeed, he views the human as made in the image of God (*imago dei*). Very impressive at first sight, and heavily endorsed by philosophers over the past two millennia.

The subtleties of these claims, though, require closer and more discerning attention. For instance, for many of the Greek fathers (inspired by Aristotle), the *imago dei* resides in the nonsexual soul, not in the fully embodied human, and much more so in the man than in the woman. And these deviations cannot be explained—as many commentators do—simply by situating Aristotle within the biology and culture of his time. For much of the two thousand years of Christendom, Aristotle has tended to be interpreted literally, and he still enjoys exalted status in scholastic philosophy; this is where things have gone drastically wrong, creating over the centuries several layers of repression, which is now being released in a range of chaotic, confused, and destructive human behaviors.

For Aristotle, the human person is endowed essentially with four characteristics. We are *autonomous*—ontologically, we each stand independently on our own;[7] we are *separate* from, and superior to, all other aspects of the material creation; we are *ensouled*—the dimension that links us with God and that no other creature has; and we are *rational*—as ensouled beings we work things out through the God-given power of reason.

In drawing up this metaphysical anthropology, Aristotle was concerned primarily with males. Females were dismissed as misbegotten males, an unfortunate demonization that St. Thomas Aquinas adopted some fifteen hundred years later, a misogyny that still haunts many of the major world religions. But what is

---

[7] Autonomy is probably the most frequently cited characteristic in the contemporary understanding of the human person. Those who promote a culture of human rights, frequently underestimating (or ignoring) responsibilities and duties, strongly emphasize human autonomy, above and beyond other characteristics, and to a degree superior to other life-forms. MacKenzie and Stoljar (2000) provide a comprehensive and carefully considered analysis of this phenomenon, highlighting that the only autonomy that will serve humanity (along with other creatures) well is a relational rather than an adversarial one.

most demeaning in Aristotle's rendition—for which he is rarely, if ever, challenged—is his allegiance to the autonomous, robust, individualistic, heroic male as the model for all responsible and holy humans. It provides a grossly distorted picture of what humans were like for much of their long evolutionary story, and also the incarnational humanity that the historical Jesus exemplifies in his life and ministry.

Because of the moralistic denunciation of the body—and its often legitimate desires—we have inherited a perverse culture where it would seem that the lid has blown off the cultural pressure cooker of repressed material, and we are engulfed with a new raw hunger that is largely misunderstood—and, therefore, falsely diagnosed. Nowhere is this more painfully manifest than in the realm of human sexuality.

Birthing in the Power of Sexuality

In the closing decades of the twentieth century, a new scandal rocked the Catholic Church, the fallout of which continues to the present time. Particularly in the white Western world, large numbers of clergy, including some bishops, were implicated in the sexual abuse of children, minors, and vulnerable adults. Stringent new measures—safeguarding—were put in place to protect potential victims, including in several cases the removal from public ministry of the alleged perpetrators, even though many were never formally charged with sexual offenses.

When reporting this scandal, public media occasionally noted that despite the seriousness of the crime, clerical sex abuse comprised less than 5 percent of all such abuse around the world. This shocking observation seems to have eluded an analysis that is long overdue and of urgent cultural import. A basic question immediately springs to mind: Why is human sexuality so problematic for so many people? Why has that God-given propensity, so full of joy, pleasure, intimacy, and creativity, become the focus of so much hurt, pain, and exploitation?

As a social scientist, I suggest that *repression* is a major part of the response to this critical, timely question. As a species we are enduring the deep-buried trauma and pain of centuries of psychosexual repression. That which should be such a liberating and empowering endowment has become a cultural and psychological nightmare for contemporary humans. And the religions—including Christianity—must shoulder the blame for much of this rampant repression.

When repression breaks out—and breaks loose—disturbing consequences are inevitable. In our time, the tinderbox of repression exploded in the 1960s. After centuries of psychosexual repression, people began to throw off their shackles within a new, reckless freedom largely driven by subconscious forces. The so-called sexual revolution articulates something of the worldwide cultural reaction to the repressed sexuality of previous centuries (a widespread sexual woundedness), but it does little to explain what was really emerging. *Evolution, not revolution, was setting the pace.* The new amorphous sexual landscape, often denounced for its promiscuity and pornography, paradoxically became a new evolutionary threshold.

One glimpses a sense of what was happening from this insightful remark by Thomas Moore: "We become inordinately absorbed in that which we neglect, and we display outlandishly what we do not deeply possess. This inversion of values, full of paradox, is a pattern that makes sense of our extreme interest in things, and our tendency at the same time to treat things badly" (1998, 243).

To find a resolution to this problem—which thus far both governments and religions seem to be avoiding—we need to revisit Aristotle (and not merely St. Augustine) to see where things went wrong in the first place. For Aristotle, human sexuality equates to biological reproduction. In a word, there is nothing to sex except biology. For Aristotle, men alone are sexual and can propagate in the power of the seed that they possess uniquely.

Women are biological organisms (misbegotten males rather than persons) whose primary purpose is to fertilize the seed on behalf of the male. Therefore, sexuality has one basic purpose: *the reproduction of the species*.

St. Thomas Aquinas criticized several aspects of Aristotle's philosophy, but it seems that Aquinas embraced and endorsed Aristotle's anthropology, even to the point of repeating the derogatory description of women as misbegotten males. The Council of Trent (1545–1563), formally declaring heterosexual monogamous marriage to be a sacrament, described its purpose as the reproduction of the species. Four hundred years later, at the Second Vatican Council, the Catholic Church changed its teaching on marriage by asserting a dual purpose: (a) the love and intimacy of the couple for each other, and (b) the reproduction of the species.[8]

This shift in the 1960s strikes me as being of enormous evolutionary significance, occurring at the same time as the explosion of the long-repressed psychosexual energy. Several new breakthroughs were happening in the 1960s, and the Catholic Church of the day seems to have well discerned the shifting focus of human sexuality. Unfortunately, the Church seems not to have kept up that discerning momentum, and with the 1968 promulgation of the papal document *Humanae Vitae* seemed to slip back toward the earlier biological understanding.

Meanwhile, the evolutionary imperative took over, and sexualized energy morphed into a range of new expressions. The evolutionary imperative I describe marks the overthrow of sexuality defined solely, or largely, as a mechanism for human reproduction. Procreation is merely one outcome of a life process with creativity as its primary focus—not just creativity among human beings, but at every level of God's creation. The energy that animates and sustains creation is channeled in the human species through our embodied sexuality.

---

[8] See *Gaudium et Spes*, chapter 1 (http://www.vatican.va).

As the repressed energy boiled over, convention was thrown to the wind, and all kinds of psychosexual experimentation ensued. The process continues to our own time, amid chaos and bewilderment but also several breakthroughs. A sense of sexual shame and guilt has largely evaporated, particularly among youth, yet millions continue to be hurt and wounded. There is an urgent cultural need to start naming the new emergence in our understanding of human sexuality today.

Let's take the example of the LGBTIQ (lesbian, gay, bisexual, transgendered, intersexed, queer) movement, epitomizing not merely new patterns of sexualized behavior, but rather *an evolutionary aspiration for an expanded horizon for the articulation and expression of human love and intimacy*. Sex is no longer the central issue; human loving, tenderness, care, and the expression of affection are the crucial factors (see Farley 2006). Searching for a gay/lesbian gene misses the bigger picture, the evolutionary imperative. Gay marriage is about a great deal more than the institution of marriage. In the desire to be more inclusive of people of other sexual orientations, we are actually redefining the very meaning of human sexuality itself.

Pertinent also to this reflection is the God we believe in, not a lone patriarchal figure (still worshiped extensively today), nor a Father-Son couple so central to our redemptive theories, but a threesome that we call the Trinity. That intense primordial relationality of the Godhead itself reflects the erotic relational dynamic of all life, humanity included. Here, perhaps, is where we need to start with a revamped theology of human sexuality.

Meanwhile, we are left with the morass of the confused and abusive sexualized landscape of our time. Let's not forget, however, that millions of people are renegotiating their way through this new landscape with remarkable wisdom and agility. We need to include them in a new ethical conversation in order to co-create a sexual morality relevant for our time.

Without this ethic we live in a moral vacuum that is undesirable from several perspectives. It is highly unlikely that religions and churches will rise to the challenge of creating these moral guidelines, because they still live and operate within the old paradigm. The new morality will need to become the responsibility of our lawmakers, and all of us casting votes for future governments need to keep this in mind.

Birthing Empowerment

Contemporary theology seems to be in pursuit of an alternative metaphor to the One who creates ex nihilo and continues to sustain creation mainly through imperial governance. That understanding of the Creator God seems to be loaded with imperial projections, instituted largely by patriarchal males. Instead, the primacy of the energizing Spirit is coming to the fore, awakening a birthing evolutionary imperative requiring a novel hermeneutic of the God who forever gives birth in and through the embodied creatures that constitute creation at large.

Without such bodies the birthing cannot take place; the creative energy of the Spirit goes nowhere. Such embodiment is the organic structure for the empowering creativity of the divine. From the vast evolving universe down to the tiny bacteria, embodiment is the royal road through which divinized becoming is facilitated. Human bodies are the latest in the evolutionary thrust of life, representing the medium of self-reflexive consciousness (that is, we can think about the fact that we can think). In us and through us the universe moves on to a higher level of becoming aware of itself and its deep sacred meaning.

Within and among humans the reservoir of the Spirit's empowering energizing is that of our sexuality. That which we have reduced to a biological mechanism for creating new human life must now be restored to its full erotic empowerment, an articulation of the Trinitarian capacity for deep and intimate interrelating, not merely among humans but throughout the entire web of universal life.

Inscribed into creation—at every level—is the birth of novel possibility, often a process of rebirth after the death of former paradigms. Embodiment is the channel for such birthing, and embodied structure enriches and empowers the divine intent. In this way we stand a better chance of understanding—theologically—the evolutionary imperative that underpins all creativity, divine and human alike. To that topic we now turn our attention.

8

The Evolutionary Imperative

While I have no doubt that the origin of life was not in fact a miracle, I do believe that we live in a bio-friendly universe of a stunningly ingenious character.

Paul Davies

The foundation of things is not so much a ground of being sustaining its existence from beneath as it is a power of attraction toward what lies ahead.

Ilia Delio

The alternative theological paradigm being explored in this book is described as an evolutionary perspective, yet the evolutionary dimension is not flagged as the first element. Rather, it falls into third place after Spirit-energy and creation as embodied birthing.

The reader may already have discerned my logic. Nothing in creation can come into being without the energetic life force of the Great Spirit. Second, we cannot describe the emergence and unfolding of evolution apart from the embodied creativity that provides, as it were, the "habitat" in which Spirit-energy flows and assumes bodily form.

Only when those two dimensions are already operative can we discern evolution at work. It is energized by the Spirit and serves as a central feature of the birthing process, inaugurating and sustaining everything that exists. Summarizing his attempted evolutionary synthesis, Jesuit theologian Roger Haight writes, "Evolution has an impact on almost every phase of human self-understanding. How could one think of God as creator and not summon up the pictures of the universe with which science now feeds our imaginations? God created our universe. To understand what that means, we have to attend to the creation that God created." He concludes, "All the disciplines dedicated to understanding the human have been revolutionized by the dynamics of evolution" (2019, 233).

Conceptual Clarity

Before proceeding, we need to note the conventional use of the term evolution, allegedly inspired by the great Charles Darwin (1809–1882).[1] Evolution describes the impact of change on the inherited characteristics of biological populations over successive generations. This process results in greater diversity at every level of biological organization, including species, individual organisms, and molecules such as DNA and proteins. Existing patterns of biodiversity have been shaped both by speciation and by extinction. Darwin (c. 1859) was the first to formulate a scientific argument for the theory of evolution by means of natural selection. The selection itself was based on the natural variety of creatures, some of which were fitter than others (hence the notion of the survival of the fittest). Geneticist Gregor Mendel (1822–1884) contributed the additional factor of genetic mutations; although genes

---

[1] Scholars writing from a more religious perspective claim that the atheistic tenor of contemporary Darwinian scholarship belongs more to the neo-Darwinians rather than to Darwin himself, as argued by theologian Elizabeth Johnson (2014).

are inherited in a predictable fashion, changes in genes can occur randomly, and they arise from environmental influences, all contributing to the notion of novelty in evolutionary developments.

In the twentieth century, the priest-paleontologist Pierre Teilhard de Chardin (1881–1955) introduced a fresh religious understanding of evolution. In fact, Teilhard's religious perspective was largely linked to the ideological superiority of the Christian religion, as understood at that time. However, his new synthesis was sufficiently robust to launch further breakthroughs—limited in scientific terms, but potentially explosive for both spirituality and theology.

An American Franciscan Sister, Ilia Delio, a theologian at Villanova University, is now emerging as the single finest exponent of Teilhard's vision and its relevance for science and cosmology in the twenty-first century. She defines evolution in these words:

> Evolution is less a mechanism than a process—a constellation of law, chance, spontaneity, and deep time. . . . Evolution is not simply a biological mechanism of gene swapping or environmental pressure. It is the unfolding and development of consciousness in which consciousness plays a significant role in the process of convergence and complexification. Evolution gives rise to religion when consciousness unfolds in a "thou-embraced-I." (2013, xvi, 98)

The evolutionary imperative I describe is not a cultural phenomenon that we can take or leave. Nor is it a movement over which we have human control. The truth is that we are being evolved, in a momentous thrust within which we allow ourselves to become an integral part of cosmic and planetary well-being, or otherwise we become increasingly alienated from life at large. I am not in any way suggesting that all is determined, and that we have no choice other than to get involved. Our coming of age is a wake-up call to realize that we are a derived species, creatures of a cosmic-planetary, co-evolutionary process in which the growth and progress of each entity—ourselves included—are only possible when we opt to integrate our becoming with that of the larger reality.

Evolution has now entered even religious discourse, and to make the concept more comprehensible for a wider audience I outlined in chapter 1 a fairly simple definition consisting of three foundational processes: growth, change, and complexity. Growth is an inescapable feature of all life-forms. Such growth is not merely about flourishing but also includes the changes involved in decay, decline, and death, which unfortunately St. Paul, in his pre-evolutionary thinking, describes as a consequence of sin. And finally, complexity describes the increasing and deeper levels of consciousness, intricacy, and mystery, evidenced in many of the scientific discoveries of the twentieth century.

I also want to introduce the notion of co-evolution, a term that describes more accurately the evolving process we explore here rather than the concept of evolution on its own. Coined by Paul R. Ehrlich and Peter H. Raven in 1964, co-evolution occurs when two or more species reciprocally affect each other's growth and development. Two or more species evolve in tandem by exerting selection pressures on each other. I adopt this wider and more intricate application to highlight the innate, collaborative orientation of every evolutionary process. Nothing can evolve in isolation; everything needs everything else.

Later in this chapter I highlight the paradoxical nature of co-evolution. It is never a case of progressive movement into greater complexity by repeating the successful models of the past (survival of the fittest). More typically it is new life and possibility emerging from chaos and breakdown, in a co-evolutionary process that cannot be rationally explained, yet the process carries deep meaning, of a depth and significance that can only be intuited from within a spiritual frame of reference.

Contrary to the rather mechanistic approach adopted by many neo-Darwinians, today the co-evolutionary process requires a multidisciplinary purview to unravel and comprehend its

impact, and within such an approach theology and spirituality
(as explored in the present work) are of central importance. In the
mid-twentieth century, Teilhard de Chardin asked, "Is evolution
a theory, a system, or a hypothesis?," and in response he wrote,
"It is much more; it is a general condition to which all theories,
all hypotheses, all systems must bow and which they must satisfy
henceforth if they are to be thinkable and true. Evolution is a
light which illuminates all facts, a curve that all lines must follow"
(1955, 219).

New Horizons

The curvature to which Teilhard refers, like the curved nature
of space-time itself, invites both classical science and former theological models into new ways of seeing and understanding. These
novel perceptions disturb the long-cherished certainties upon
which dogmatic truths thrived and patriarchal power triumphed.
These sturdy artifacts, purporting to uphold eternal truth, are no
longer as secure as they once were; in fact, many of them are
shaking in the wind and are unlikely to endure the storms of
postmodernity.

The Spell of Solidity

According to Carter Phipps, "We have been captivated by the
spell of solidity, the fallacy of fixity, the illusion of immobility, the
semblance of stasis. . . . No longer the victims of unchangeable
circumstances, trapped in a pre-given universe, we find ourselves
released into a vast, open-ended process—one that is malleable,
changeable, subject to uncertainty and chance, perhaps, but also,
in small but not insignificant ways, responsive to our choices and
actions" (2012, 28, 30).

The God whom we have long considered to be the unmoved
mover has lost his place in this emerging worldview. In our day of
mass information, in which millions distrust wisdom handed down

from on high and accommodate mobility and fluidity in daily life, faith in this never-changing God is in rapid and irreversible decline. For some it results in the abandonment of religion, but since creatures of Spirit cannot long endure without spiritual meaning, frequently the outcome is displacement rather than abandonment. The pursuits of power, addictive consumerism, and hedonistic escape are just some of the compensatory gods we have adopted.

The religions are quick to condemn the reckless postmodern abandonment of the former solidity, but are quite weak at discerning either the nature of what is transforming or the alternatives that are being pursued. While mainline religion is in decline—with some notable exceptions such as Christian Pentecostalism and Islamic fundamentalism—an amorphous spiritual awakening is emerging among millions of spiritual seekers today. The unmoved mover is struggling to survive, but the mobile Spirit once more breathes across the chaos of creation (cf. Gen 1), re-creating novel possibilities for science and theology alike.

Sense of Direction

The major world religions tend to view directionality either in cyclical or linear fashion. The great Eastern religions—notably Hinduism, Buddhism, and Sikhism—view life in terms of repeating cycles until one eventually reaches the ultimate state of fulfillment: nirvana. The monotheistic religions—Judaism, Christianity, and Islam—postulate an original creation and a grand finale at some future point, when all will be consummated into the fullness of divine life. For much of Christian history, the end of all things (the end of the world) was perceived to be a cataclysmic event, often associated with the notion of apocalypse. Throughout the twentieth century, attention shifted toward eschatology, denoting a hope-filled fulfillment in which God would become all-in-all, with the material creation itself enduring in some radically refashioned way.

As already indicated, science informs theology today to a degree largely unknown in previous times. Science frequently opens up deeper levels of mystery and truth beyond conventional religious understandings. When it comes to evolution, the churches have long opposed the neo-Darwinians, for whom evolution is a random force without a predictable sense of direction. It resembles a blind battle of wits in which the strong win and the weak lose. The renowned Stephen J. Gould endorsed this view, but toward the end of his life conceded that while he could not entertain the notion of purpose in evolution, he would accept that it had a preferred sense of direction. At this juncture theology and science enter quite a fertile dialogue, although only engaging a few theologians to date, such as the Distinguished Research Professor of Georgetown University, John F. Haught.

For Haught, it is the lure of the future more than anything else that informs the evolutionary imperative. To the best of my knowledge, the philosopher Karl Popper was the first to articulate this understanding of evolution. It has been expanded and explained in greater detail in several of the written works of John F. Haught (2010; 2015). According to Haught, "Evolution, viewed theologically, means that creation is still happening and that God is creating and saving the world not a retro, that is, by pushing it forward out of the past, but ab ante, by calling it from up ahead" (2015, 52). Theologically, I understand that the central attraction of the lure of the future is a fruit and wisdom of the Holy Spirit.[2]

The rational linear approach, so favored in Scholastic thought, is just too simplistic for the complex threshold of modern evolution. In the entangled space-time world of quantum physics, past, present, and future are intimately intertwined. The present moment is an eternal now, informed not merely by what we learn from the past but also by what we anticipate from the future.

---

[2] The lure of the Spirit is hereby understood as essentially creative and open to new possibilities. Traditionally, theology tends to follow the Darwinian view that wisdom from the past is more substantial and reliable, while the lure of the Spirit invites us to embrace God's revealing truth as primarily informed with future hope and surprise.

Driven by Consciousness

Back in 1931 renowned physicist Max Planck observed that consciousness is the fundamental stuff of all creation, and that matter is derived therefrom. In this context, consciousness denotes information as a driving energetic force (see Currivan 2017, 2–20). It is not merely an endowment of human intelligence, but an empowering quality of creation in all its aspects and at every stage of its long historical unfolding. Aliveness, therefore, can no longer be reserved to human beings, nor can the human form of aliveness be deemed superior to all other forms. On the contrary, we know that everything that constitutes our embodiment as earthlings, including our capacity for conscious thought, is given to us from the earth, itself a living organism, energized from the larger cosmic web of life, as brilliantly outlined by British scientist Tom Oliver (2020).

But from where does the cosmic creation obtain this resourcefulness? Once more we are called to transcend inherited academic distinctions and transgress the rationality that has been so foundational to our inherited understandings. We move to a higher level of discourse, in pursuit of a deeper integration. In theological terms (as indicated in chapter 6 of this volume), it is the Holy Spirit who enlivens all that exists (cf. Boff 2015; Haughey 2015). For the Christian religion, so long stuck in the dualistic split between the sacred and secular, this innate sacredness calls forth a range of new challenges, particularly pertinent to the threatened ecological status of our earth today.

The all-embracing sense of aliveness unfolds along an evolutionary trajectory that transcends simple cause-and-effect, with a sense of direction that is open and unpredictable, always evolving into greater complexity (for further elaboration, see Delio 2015 and Stewart 2000). The culture of patriarchal certainty and hierarchical ordering (as evidenced in several religious doctrines) is increasingly understood as an anthropocentric projection that alienates humans by separating us from the womb of our becoming and attributing to us an elevated status increasingly viewed as exploitative and dangerous. We have ended up with a perverted anthropology that has seriously distorted how we perceive and understand several elements of faith, including our Christian understanding of incarnation.

Imbued with Paradox

By postulating a consciousness-driven creation, probably fueled by a spirit-infused creative energy, we are reframing rather than denying the chanciness that the neo-Darwinians claim is inherent to creation at large. Without this chanciness there is in fact no room for creativity or freedom. Certain levels of negative fallout are inevitable, but in the context of consciousness they take on a much more complex yet coherent meaning, central to which is the notion of paradox.

As already indicated in chapter 5, creation's evolutionary unfolding is endowed with the paradoxical interplay of creation-cum-destruction, an unceasing cyclical rhythm of birth-death-rebirth. Major religions tend to dismiss this paradox as a fundamental flaw requiring divine salvific intervention, particularly through the death and resurrection of the historical Jesus. This enduring paradox is central to the entire fabric of universal life. It includes those puzzling and at times frightening features like pain, suffering, calamity, earthquakes, breakdown, decline, and death. These are not evils to be eliminated; they are foundational to all growth, change, and complexity throughout the entire creation.[3]

The religious believer will ask: Is this how God created the world? Did the same God also create the paradoxes that characterize our creation? To the religionist, a positive response undermines everything one has learned to believe about the impassable,

---

[3] See the earthquake example in chapter 5 of this volume.

all-powerful, metaphysical God. And for the classical scientist, it
feels like too much of a contradiction to accept that the creative
life force—divine or otherwise—is also the source and sustenance
of destruction. We are dealing with something bigger and deeper
than contradiction, namely paradox.[4] This paradox is the foundation for freedom and creativity. Without the paradox, all we have
left is total nihilism.

Central to these reflections is the role that death plays in the
grand scheme of things. Every major religion has considered death
as an evil to overcome and eliminate. In a co-evolutionary universe, we need to view death, decay, and decline in a much more
integrated way. The need to befriend death is an essential feature
of all growth and development. It is the human denunciation of
death, and our addictive drives to get rid of it, that cause enormous
amounts of meaningless suffering throughout the world today.

Lateral Thinking

Much of Christian theology and the ensuing spirituality are
defined and described in terms of classical Greek metaphysics,
rational thought, and logical argument. It is a linear, sequential
process favored by dominant males seeking control and mastery
through rational discourse. This strategy is alien to evolutionary
unfolding, lacking in the creativity, imagination, and intuition necessary for us to apprehend the complexities of this age and every
other. Beyond the traditional affiliation with Scholastic philosophy, theology must now embrace a multidisciplinary dynamic to
engage the lateral consciousness of the twenty-first century and
the coming-of-age that is required if we are to engage the new
emergencies of our time.

---

[4] I refer the reader to the inspiring contemplation on the meaning of *paradox* in Miriam Therese Winter (2009). For further reading,
see Bernard Tickerhoof (2002). For a more mystical perspective, see
Cyprian Smith (1987).

This lateral unfolding is cyclic in nature rather than linear. It does not begin with some ideal past moment when everything was harmonious and complete, nor does it embrace the notion of an end time, a once-and-forever culmination. In this understanding there was never a time when human nature was intact and sinless. Therefore, there was never a fall from grace. Had humans not the freedom to use their creativity—and make mistakes in the process—then we would not be the complex, evolved creatures we are today.

Several theological conundrums arise here. In terms of anthropology (what it means to be human), we perceive an open-ended way of being human, as creatures forever in process—not merely creatures who attain higher faculties because of the type of brain we are inhabiting,[5] or organisms destined to become a final "product" whether in this life or in the next. Regarding soteriology (salvation and redemption), if we are not fundamentally flawed (through original sin, etc.), then we don't need a divine rescue. We are not saved merely by the power of the cross, but by a divine empowerment forever seeking to transform our human efforts, warts and all. Finally, Christology (Jesus as the Christ) itself needs to be viewed in evolutionary terms (as I attempted to do in previous works: O'Murchu 2008; 2017). If Jesus is for us the human face of God made radically visible on earth, then it is our own

---

[5] According to American neuroscientist Paul MacLean, the hierarchical organization of the human brain represents the gradual acquisition of the brain structures through evolution. The triune brain model suggests first the emergence of the reptilian brain some 220 million years ago, which is thought to be in charge of our primal instincts. This was followed some 125 million years ago by the limbic system, which is in charge of our emotions or affective system. Finally comes the neocortex, merely 3 million years ago, which is thought to be responsible for rational or objective thought. Such brain developments certainly indicate a growth in complexity but fail to capture more subtle evolutionary dynamics whereby we humans, throughout our long evolutionary story, have been using our brains in what seems to have been highly creative modes.

evolutionary story—over some 7 million years—that illuminates the divine visibility.

Jesus does not come to rescue us from anything, because in evolutionary terms we "got it right" most of the time, in the sense of behaving creatively and responsibly. This more wholesome outcome came about precisely because we remained very close to the earth and were therefore more attuned to the grace of God as the Great Spirit. Instead, the historical Jesus (for us Christians) serves as an affirmation, confirmation, and celebration of all that we have achieved as evolutionary beings, while simultaneously embodying a future sense of direction for our ongoing evolution. A whole new Christology needs to be created.

Cooperation

Evolution is not solely dependent on the survival of the fittest, but rather on the triumph of cooperation. For John Stewart, cooperation is evolution's arrow: "Co-operators will inherit the earth, and eventually the universe" (2000, 8). However, it has to be a quality of cooperation that can embrace and integrate legitimate self-interest as purported in both Judaism and Christianity: Love God! And to do that, one has to love the neighbor, which is genuinely possible only when we learn to love ourselves (cf. Lev 19:18; Mk 12:29–30). Genuine self-interest is not contrary to faith in God nor to faith in evolution; it is the prerequisite for both.

Our evolutionary growth is largely determined by the quality of our engagement with the process of life. While biologists often claim that evolution only progresses at the level of individuals and through innately selfish and conflictual behavior, physicist Jude Currivan observes that "a growing number of researchers are arguing instead for a more inclusive multilevel approach that recognizes the evolutionary effects of group cooperation and altruism" (2017, 225).

Several scientific developments of the twentieth century have surfaced cooperation as a foundational dimension not merely of human flourishing but of the creative drive inherent to all evolutionary processes. I cite four examples to illustrate a shift from the emphasis on competition and combat to that of cooperation and communal impetus.[6]

I begin with Russian physical chemist and Nobel laureate Ilya Prigogine (1917–2003), considered one of the founders of complexity science, who was awarded the Nobel Prize for chemistry in 1977 for his work on the thermodynamics of nonequilibrium systems. His seminal book, *Order Out of Chaos: Man's New Dialogue with Nature* (Prigogine and Stengers 1984), shows how the two great themes of classical science, order and chaos—which coexisted uneasily for centuries—are being reconciled in a new and unexpected synthesis. Beyond the tyranny of entropy is a deeper and more enduring sense of order.

Second, this latent ordered harmony has been raised to a new level of comprehension with the pioneering work of American evolutionary theorist Lynn Margulis (1938–2011) through the notion of symbiogenesis.[7] According to Margulis our prevailing view of evolution as chronic, bloody competition among individuals and species is a popular distortion of Darwin's notion of survival of the fittest. It now gives way to a new view of continual cooperation, strong interaction, and mutual dependence among

---

[6] In recent years, several studies highlight the central role of cooperation in human flourishing. For a public readership I recommend Jeremy Rifkin (2009), Sarah Blaffer Hrdy (2009), and Patrik Lindenfors (2017).

[7] *Symbiogenesis* literally means *becoming by living together.* More than eighty years ago, before we knew much about the structure of cells, Russian botanist Boris Kozo-Polyansky brilliantly outlined the concept of symbiogenesis, the symbiotic origin of cells with nuclei. This theory has been further advanced and substantiated with microbiological evidence by Lynn Margulis.

life-forms. Life did not take over the globe by combat, but by networking (more in Margulis and Sagan 1997).

Third, I allude briefly to the pioneering work of British primatologist and anthropologist Jane Goodall (b. 1934). Considered to be the world's foremost expert on chimpanzees, Goodall is best known for her long study of social and family interactions of wild chimpanzees at the Gombe National Park in Tanzania. Her extensive and intimate study of chimps illuminates the behavior and lifestyle of our closest living relatives, revealing that, like humans, chimps build tools, have unique personalities, and even wage wars. Despite the obvious violence and conflict, what is most compelling in Goodall's research is the extensive cooperation that prevails among our primate ancestors.

Finally, such innate programming for cooperation is also evidenced in the brain research of Sebastian Seung, a Princeton-based, multidisciplinary Korean American researcher covering the fields of neuroscience, physics, and bioinformatics. According to his connectome theory, our brains function in a highly synchronized fashion, programmed primarily for cooperation rather than adversarial conflict. Seung's book *Connectome: How the Brain's Wiring Makes Us Who We Are* (2012) elaborates further on a promising vision, with substantial theological as well as scientific implications.

Beyond the Religious-Scientific Collusion

Canadian mathematician and biologist Brian Goodwin (1931–2009) is considered to be a controversial and original researcher in what is often described as the "new biology." While Darwinism stresses conflict and competition, the new biology advocates the more creative outcomes arising from cooperation and altruistic behavior. In his popular book *How the Leopard Changed Its Spots: The Evolution of Complexity* (1994), Goodwin provides a fascinating outline indicating that both science and religion are trapped in a very similar ideology, upholding a pessimistic and debilitating view of life.

This is Goodwin's formulation (1994, 29–30):

Darwinian Principles	Religious Principles
Organisms are constructed by groups of genes whose goal is to leave more copies of themselves. The hereditary material is basically "selfish."	Human beings are born in sin and they perpetuate it in sexual reproduction, Greed and pride are basic elements of that flawed sinful condition.
The inherent selfish qualities of the hereditary material are reflected in the competitive interactions between organisms, resulting in the survival of the fittest.	Humanity, therefore, is condemned to a life of conflict and perpetual toil in the desire to improve one's lot in life.
Organisms constantly are trying to improve and outdo weaker elements, but the landscape of evolution keeps changing, so the struggle is endless, as in Steven Weinberg's "hostile universe."	Humanity's effort at improvement is jeopardized by the imperfect, sinful world in which we have been placed. The struggle never ends.
Paradoxically, human beings can develop altruistic qualities that contradict their inherently selfish nature, by means of education and other cultural efforts.	But, by faith and moral effort humanity can be saved from its fallen, selfish state, normally requiring the intervention of an external divine rescuer.

For the human, both science and theology seek a way out, a new freedom, but their respective strategies stand little hope of delivering such liberation, since their proposed remedies are too rationalistic, anthropocentric, and deprived of the creative empowerment upon which evolution has thrived and flourished from time immemorial. An evolutionary perspective requires a very different approach to theology from that of the two previous paradigms outlined in this book. Our starting point is the cosmic narrative, a transhuman vision beyond our controlling anthropocentrism, a relational Trinitarian dynamism rather than an individualized imperial ruling divinity, a sense of faith in which we trust God's loving providence rather than one defined by metaphysical qualities or denounced by rational atheism.

The Anthropological Shift

The evolutionary perspective changes our way of seeing everything. For the present work, however, the implications for human nature and our understanding of the place of the human are of central importance. In the old paradigm, humans are God's primary concern, the only life-form that can reveal God's project for creation. In the ensuing narrative, however, humans erred (sinned), and from there on both scripture and theology are preoccupied with only one thing: the redemption of the human.

But what kind of humanity is theology seeking to redeem, and what does such redemption deliver? According to French theorist René Girard (in a view favored by a substantial number of mainline theologians), Jesus in the power of the cross destroys violent scapegoating forever. Clearly, the history of Christianity (and of all other world religions) does not vouch for such an outcome. In the name of Jesus and his cross, we have maimed and butchered, oppressed and even exterminated those who disagree with us. And the Judeo-Christian faith has failed creation rather dismally, particularly due to dualistic splitting (e.g., the sacred vs. the secular).

Consequently, the prevailing anthropology has now become bankrupt, and unfortunately continues to corrupt any meaningful empowering sense of the Christian faith. Our conventional anthropology is based on the highly individualized, separate, rational being (the male of the species, since in this paradigm— according to Aristotle, St. Thomas Aquinas, and a long line of eminent philosophers—females are deemed to be misbegotten males). The words *separate* and *rational* carry enormous cultural and theological weight, with meanings that have often eluded both philosophers and theologians.

Separate here denotes away from, and over against, the material creation. Humans, being endowed with souls, are rated higher than any other creature in creation, and are destined to operate from a more exalted status, contrary and superior to everything in the material creation. In traditional Christianity, therefore, the primary purpose of a spiritual life was to enable the person to save the immortal soul, so that at death it could escape from this vale of tears, to the fulfillment of a world beyond this material creation. Now that we are seeking to reclaim our primary identity as earthlings, and no longer believe in a world "beyond" (since nothing exists outside our cosmic creation), the notion of the human as a separate, superior entity makes no sense, anthropologically or theologically.

Rationality is a quality long cherished by all schools of philosophy and is of particular significance for the Christian Scholastic tradition. We work out the meaning of life and reach the truth through the power of reason (a capacity that in Aristotelian anthropology is only possessed by the male). This is a deluded claim, a philosophical and theological liability, which has had a highly destructive impact on human civilization generally. It reinforces the separation from, and superiority to, creation, and it also leads to the suppression—and repression—of other key human qualities, indeed, the very ones that make us unique as a species: imagination, intuition, consciousness, and creativity.

Throughout the course of the twentieth century, thanks to the growing popularity of paleontology and of social sciences such as psychology and anthropology, a very different understanding of human personhood came into focus. In fact, it had already flourished in several ancient and modern indigenous cultures. We encapsulate its meaning in the oft-cited words: I am at all times the sum of my relationships, and that is what confers my personal identity. It is often described as a relational anthropology.

The Trinity in Evolutionary Context

This relational horizon evokes an evolutionary perspective not merely for how we understand our humanity (anthropology), but everything else in life as well. It is also a core dimension of the doctrine of the Trinity, with its parallels in several of the great world religions and, according to Cynthia Bourgeault (2014), a rootedness in ancient esoteric wisdom. Beyond the complex metaphysical rhetoric of the early church councils, theologians throughout the closing decades of the twentieth century began to redefine our understanding of the Trinity more in relational than metaphysical terms.[8]

Beyond the mathematical quagmire of trying to fit three into one, and the patriarchal ordering of Father, Son, and Holy Spirit, this doctrine seems to embody an archetypal intuition asserting that the more foundational nature of God is a process of relationality. I suggest that the challenge of such a doctrine is not so much in its dense philosophical or theological intelligibility, but rather in our attempt to discern the underlying experience of the mystery of God that led to the doctrinal articulation in the first place. The fact that this doctrine arises in all the world's major religions should alert us to a deeper universal truth. Worthy of note too is the observation of scientist George Greenstein (1988) that configurations of three occur frequently throughout the galactic and planetary realms.

We can only speculate how our ancient ancestors in deep time experienced the sense of divine mystery within and around them. As we delve deeper into our paleontological and anthropological story, our sense of interconnectedness with all aspects of the web of life is now well beyond mere speculation. Interrelatedness defines so many of our ancient ways of seeing and understand-

---

[8] For a valuable overview, see Elizabeth Johnson (2007, 202–25); also Ruben L. F. Habito in Tan and Tran (2016, 161–81). For a more comprehensive overview, see Joseph Bracken (2014).

ing. Did our ancient ancestors come to a conclusion, not once but several times, that whatever else the divine mystery is about, it denotes above all else a deep capacity for interrelatedness?[9] Thousands of years later, the experience morphs into a formal doctrine that the churches name as the Trinity.

This return to an underlying and enduring sense of deep relationship, as a foundational aspect of the Godhead, features in the work of several Trinitarian theologians in recent decades (Catherine LaCugna, Patricia Fox, John Zizioulas). Nonetheless, an individualized understanding of God still dominates in both the spiritual and theological landscapes. It still seems quite unclear how the relational understanding can be translated into daily faith, conceptually and practically.

In our desire to retain a personalist understanding and appropriation of God, we inevitably adopt a set of anthropomorphic attributes. Paradoxically, this undermines the rich potential of the relational matrix rather than enhancing it. As indicated in previous chapters, there seems to be a significant swing toward the priority of the Spirit in our emerging understanding of the divine at work in creation. Not merely does this require a reorganizing of the traditional Trinitarian triad of Father, Son, and Holy Spirit—more importantly, it engenders a whole new understanding of the divine mystery at work in our world as well as in our own lives.

As conceptualized by indigenous peoples around the world, the notion of the Great Spirit is not personal in our normal adoption of that quality as used in religious language. Because of past dualistic indoctrination, we all too quickly conclude that we are dealing with a cold impersonal encounter, largely devoid of personalist significance. But this is not how indigenous peoples experience the Great Spirit. They neither think nor feel in dualistic, binary distinctions. The Spirit that inhabits and energizes

---

[9] It might also be possible that our ancestors understood God as a *divine insistence* (a fertile mystical notion developed by theologian John Caputo [2013]).

everything in creation is a life force that embraces all that is deeply human, while simultaneously transcending all our human categorizations.

As indicated in chapter 6, with the Spirit taking priority, the notion of the Creative Father, operating ex nihilo, must now be reenvisioned in a major way. This is a long-overdue corrective to the patriarchal portrayal of God, which features to one degree or another in all the major religions. Empowering birthing rather than patriarchal governance now becomes the more generic metaphor.

Effectively, this ensues with Jesus falling into third place, which for the vast majority of Christian theologians feels like an out-and-out betrayal, and therefore is totally unacceptable. The problem, I suggest, is not this recasting of Jesus but the difficulty in reenvisioning the meaning of Jesus outside the traditional Trinitarian construct. In every evolutionary breakthrough, we believe there has been a divine affirmation and celebration of the new breakthrough. I suggest that this is where Jesus, as the incarnational face of God on earth, comes truly into his own. With the emergence of humans as the latest evolutionary newcomers, a new manifestation of God to accompany this emergence makes a great deal of spiritual and theological sense.

It means, of course, that the incarnation of God in the human does not happen for the first time in and through Jesus of Nazareth. Rather the initial and foundational incarnation in the human first happens in East Africa some 7 million years ago. And the God who incarnated uniquely in us—7 million years ago—is that same God who accompanies the human through the long evolutionary maturation over those several eons. Then comes the appearance of Jesus of Nazareth as the affirmation, confirmation, and celebration of all we achieved throughout that time, while also serving as an embodied wisdom of what we are yet to become at the further stages of this evolutionary trajectory.

Another objection to this reenvisioning of the meaning of Jesus is that it seems to confine Jesus merely to human reality, whereas conventional Christianity has long cherished the belief that Jesus relates to the whole of creation. This link with the wider creation can still be maintained, even in a more integrated way, when we remember that in our long evolutionary journey, we humans were deeply embedded in the earth. In fact, this deep earthiness made us into the uniquely creative creatures that we are. In this way, Jesus, the human, along with the earthly creation itself, is insinuated into a deeply transpersonal force for empowering transformation.

Faith in an Evolutionary God

Whether one agrees or disagrees with these ideas, we cannot bypass the depth and significance of our human evolutionary story within the larger story of all that has evolved—and continues to do so—on our earth. Evolution is an inescapable fact of life, and it would seem an inescapable dimension of how God relates to all creation. When we embrace the evolutionary imperative, inevitably the metaphysical construal of God, and its limited time context of a mere two thousand years, simply will not stand up to the test of a deeper and broader discernment. For John Caputo, "Physics is all the metaphysics we are going to get. . . . Physics has philosophy on the run" (2013, 189, 194).

These evolutionary propensities mark a seismic shift from a worldview in which we were "captivated by the spell of solidity, the fallacy of fixity, the illusion of immobility, the semblance of stasis," as described by Phipps (2012, 26), who goes on to say, "but the evolution revolution is starting to break that spell. We are realizing that we are, in fact, not standing on solid ground. But neither are we adrift in a meaningless universe. . . . We are part and parcel of a vast process of becoming."

Perhaps one of the biggest challenges of that process is the realization that we are not in charge. We are beneficiaries of an evolutionary process, not its masters. As creatures blessed with the gift of reflexive consciousness, we are creation becoming more deeply aware of itself. For our species this is a new threshold of consciousness—not another resource that will enhance our anthropocentric drive to conquer and control, but one making ever more transparent our place as a servant species, whose happiness and fulfillment are only possible when we choose to co-evolve with all the other organisms with which we share the web of life.

Our place in the scheme of things has to be reconsidered—and significantly reframed. In turn that will require a fresh reenvisioning of how God desires our incarnational identity, as embodied creatures in an embodied earth. That becomes the topic for our next chapter.

Empowering Incarnation

*That God cannot be embodied, except in the
ecclesiastically controlled, historical event of an
individual man from Nazareth is hubris of the
highest degree.*

Laurel C. Schneider

*As human beings we all have a quantum nature,
a pure and coherent nature which bestows upon
us the right—and responsibility—to consciously
realize it as best we are able. The benefits of
realizing our quantum nature are as boundless
as the potentials intrinsic to the quantum itself.*

Paul Levy

For many readers, I expect that one of the most jolting and disturbing features of the new theological paradigm under consid-
eration in this book is the relocation of Jesus and the Christian
story. Throughout the centuries, theology begins with Jesus, the
primary and definitive revelation of God for us. Any diminution
of this absolute priority is generally considered to be heretical
relativism at its worst, a serious betrayal of the one and only revelation of ultimate truth.

Consequently, most attempts at multifaith dialogue ever since the mid-twentieth century, or the more recent emergence of comparative theology (Clooney 2010), consistently falter around the Christian insistence on the uniqueness of Jesus. In truth it is not the uniqueness of Jesus that is at stake—a feature that is not at risk in the new paradigm—but rather the power we attribute to Jesus. It is the fear that we might compromise this unilateral omnipotence, the might of the reigning God that validates all forms of patriarchal power on earth. It feels like an irrational preoccupation with the preservation and promotion of such power. The real issue, it seems to me, is not the power of truth, but the truth of power.

Whither Deep Incarnation?

In a book titled *Deep Incarnation* (Edwards 2019), completed shortly before his death in 2019, Australian scholar Denis Edwards collated a range of emerging ideas on the notion of deep incarnation. Building on the foundational work of scholars such as Niels Henrik Gregersen (2015), Elizabeth Johnson (2014), Celia Deane-Drummond (2009; 2017), Christopher Southgate (2008), and Karl Rahner (1978), and integrating corresponding insights from ancient Christian sources in Irenaeus and Athanasius, Edwards offers the following definition of this expanded notion of incarnation:

> The incarnation not only weds Jesus to humanity but also reaches beyond humanity to all living creatures and to the cosmic dust of which all earth creatures are composed. In this way . . . matter and flesh become part of God's own story forever. The incarnation is a cosmic event. . . . The incarnation is transformative for the whole creation because of the loving self-identification of the crucified Christ with creation, in its disharmony and decay as well

as its profusion and vitality, and because the risen Christ
draws the whole creation with him into the eschatological newness of resurrection. (2019, 6, 111)

For Edwards, and for all the sources he quotes, incarnation belongs
primarily to the story of Jesus in the context of the Christian faith.
Foundationally, incarnation equals Jesus. He then goes on to
explore how we can extend that particular, primary understanding
to embrace the wider dimensions of creation so that we can come
to see that the incarnation, primarily embodied in and mediated
through Jesus, can also embrace and be inclusive of all dimensions
of God's creation.[1]

Like many other theologians, Edwards seeks to honor the
primacy of Jesus as the Christ, as understood within the Christian
notion of the Trinity. While he endorses the need for an expanded
understanding of the Holy Spirit (2019, 106–10), Edwards retains
the traditional Trinitarian hierarchy of Father, Son, and Holy
Spirit. While admirable in its desire to expand and deepen what
Christians at one time tried to reserve exclusively to the Christian
religion, the notion of *deep incarnation,* as developed by Denis
Edwards (and the sources he cites), falls well short of the theological horizons engaging our attention today.

Consider, for example, this challenge from theologian David
Tracy (1994). Tracy claims that with the emergence of postmodernity, *theos* had finally returned to unsettle the dominance of

---

[1] In support of his argument, Edwards quotes from the Roman
document *Dominum et Vivificantem* of 1986, written by the late Pope
John Paul II: "The Incarnation of God the Son signifies the taking up
into unity with God not only of human nature, but in this human
nature, in a sense, of everything that is 'flesh': the whole of humanity,
the entire visible and material world. The Incarnation then also has a
cosmic significance, a cosmic dimension. The 'first born of all creation'
becoming incarnate in the individual humanity of Christ, unites himself
in some way with the entire reality of the human, which is also 'flesh'
and in this reality with all 'flesh,' with the whole of creation" (para. 50).

modern *logos*, a kind of repressive rationalism that had prevailed for centuries. Good theology needs both *theos* and *logos*, but frequently one has been overemphasized to the detriment of the other. Moreover, a third variant has been largely suppressed— namely *pathos*, the God who is immersed in the passionate and painful desire for a better world, and not one metaphysically suspended from the messy reality of daily life. In fact we need to go further and embrace an even more complex phenomenon, namely *eros,* as outlined by contemporary authors such as F. LeRon Shults and Jan-Olav Henriksen (2011).

Central to a broader understanding of incarnation is the notion of *embodiment*. As suggested in an earlier work (O'Murchu 2017), I believe this is where our revamped understanding of incarnation needs to begin. No longer do people accept that the only authentic embodiment of God in our midst happened in and through the historical Jesus, nor can they accept that Jesus is the one and only person who has ever had the experience of being incarnated. Such a belief is untenable in an evolutionary universe.

When Jesus is understood as the primary, if not the exclusive, embodiment of incarnation, then inevitably humans are deemed to be the primary beneficiaries of such a God-given endowment. In doing theology today, we try to honor creation itself as God's primary revelation to us, the divine creativity at work throughout the universe for billions of years long before humans, religions, or churches ever came to be. In the embodiment of creation itself God has been incarnate for billions of years, and creation's own multiple bodies are the vehicles through which the creative energy of the divine flows and matures into a vast range of expressions. Nor should such corporeal beings be reduced to human corporeality; it is not appropriate anymore to view the human body as superior to all other embodied forms.

All forms of embodiment—from bacteria to the universe— evidence a God who loves bodies and chooses the corporeal form in every initiative of co-creation. Everything in creation grows and flourishes in an embodied context. While Spirit represents the energetic life force of everything in creation, clearly the body is the medium through which Spirit-power evolves and flourishes. Thus we discern the deep wisdom in this observation from naturalist-cum-philosopher David Abram: "The body is a place where clouds, earthworms, guitars, clucking hens, and clear-cut hillside all converge, forging alliances, mergers, and metamorphoses. . . . The body itself is a kind of place—not a solid object but a terrain through which things pass and in which they sometimes settle and sediment" (2010, 229–30). *The body is a process rather than a product*, an evolving and expanding horizon within which various elements seek out a more optimal climate for growth and flourishing.

We now revisit the material of chapter 5 above, on the Great Spirit, the primary energizing force at work in creation. I suggest we should consider the Great Spirit, and not Jesus, to be the foundational, archetypal articulation of God at work in creation. And this embodiment of the divine is not some transcendent, ethereal phenomenon above and beyond the material creation. To the contrary, it is the living earth itself as a vibrating, dynamic organism, energized by the creative energy of the Great Spirit. In other words, the revealed truth and presence of the divine reach us through the living earth itself. Our earthiness is the umbilical cord linking us to the source of our holiness (read: wholeness), through the earth, not in spite of it, and certainly not beyond it. In a word, our earthiness is the royal road to deep incarnation.

Thus far, I am suggesting that the Great Spirit, as understood in First Nations spirituality, should be considered the primary embodiment of God in our created universe. Second, our earth-embodiment, informed by the insights of Gaia theory (James Lovelock), suggests a complex and intelligent organic process that has direction and purpose deeply inscribed in its daily workings. Long before humans came on the scene, the incarnation of Holy Wisdom was at work in planet Earth itself—leading inevitably (it seems to me) to the evolution of organic life.

The Spirit is infused in every aspect of creation as its creative and sustaining energy. Without body, however, the Spirit goes nowhere; *it is in and through bodies that Spirit becomes grounded and generic at every level of creation's evolution.* Here we are confronting a major shift of emphasis. Throughout modern human civilization the human is regarded as a superior being, an inflated status fully supported by the formal religions, which claim that the human incarnates the divine on earth above and beyond any other organic creature. In fact, religionists of a more fundamental persuasion claim that it is only in and through the human that God becomes incarnate on earth.

If the Great Spirit is the foundational articulation of divine embodiment—the central feature of deep incarnation—then we need to reconsider what it means to be human within a revamped Christology. The anthropological context needs substantial attention and discernment. If Jesus represents a new breakthrough for the human species, traditionally described in terms of salvation and redemption, why reduce it to a mere two thousand years ago, when humanity has flourished over a time span of *several million* years? And why do we associate Jesus so exclusively with the negative, sinful side, when our long evolutionary story illuminates so many other capacities?

Embodiment Reenvisioned

Thus, Christianity's manner of making contact with the most basic physical, biological processes, is through an inclusive radical interpretation of its doctrine of the Incarnation, not now merely in one human being, Jesus of Nazareth, but in the world as God's body. . . . God is always incarnate, always bound to the world as its lover, as close to it as we are to our own bodies, and concerned before all else to see that the body, God's world, flourishes.

Sallie McFague

The Christian concept of incarnation has changed dramatically since the mid-twentieth century. Long associated with the coming of Jesus to rescue and redeem humanity, *incarnation* described the unique way in which the historical Jesus was born, grew up, ministered publicly, was crucified, and rose from the dead. And no other religious leader achieved that outcome as perfectly as Jesus, who therefore has been declared as the Savior not just of Christians but of all humans.

In the new paradigm, the power shifts significantly, along with our discernment of truth. We begin with the revelatory wisdom of God's creation, predating humanity, along with all our religious constructs, by billions of years. Jesuit theologian Roger Haight states the challenge as follows: "One cannot imagine a more magnificent and yet more intimate formula of incarnation than creation. . . . Creation provides the basis for God within. Creation affirmed in the context of an immense universe and a quiet experience of God within the self, provides the foundation for the meaningfulness of the term *incarnation* today" (2019, 187, emphasis in original). We need to begin where God begins in time—and that is with the cosmic, universal creation. It is in contemplating the nature and meaning of that creation that we come to apprehend and discern the creative life force that brings into being and sustains the entire cosmic adventure.

My suggested strategy for that discernment—as outlined thus far in this book—is to seek out those primordial movements of divine creativity. Science names the foundational stuff as *energy*[2]—not the quantifiable type capable of being measured and explained by classical physics, but that which emanates from the creative vacuum, the fertile emptiness, interweaving its way and eventually morphing into the generative dynamics that uphold the universe

---

[2] Theologian Gordon Kaufman (2004) names it *creativity*, while Holmes Rolston III (1999) names it *fertility, fecundity, generative capacity.*

and augment its evolutionary growth and expansion. That birthing forth from the Spirit-inspired energy we traditionally attribute to God the Father, the supreme creator.

In the new paradigm, we do not begin with the patriarchal creator, but instead with the energizing Spirit, without whose creative energy the creator cannot create.[3] And the creative impetus—the empowering energy of the Spirit—is mediated through bodies. The process of embodiment seems to be God's favored mode for the evolution, complexification, and incarnation of creation.[4] It is from within that embodied context that we explore anew the Christian notion of incarnation.

Only when we do justice to that vastly profound evolutionary unfolding can we honor the foundational mystery we name as God, and then discern how that God manifests in and through our human embodied state. But that, too, requires a further caution. Embodiment does not begin with us humans. It begins with the vastly evolving universe—a world without beginning or end—and is realized in us humans, not through some special endowment called a soul, but through a well-integrated affiliation with our status as earthlings. Theologian Oliver Davies states, "The new scientific self-understanding prompts us to think of ourselves as being not only *in* the world, as subject, but simultaneously to think of ourselves, indeed more correctly still, as *being* world. . . . We are creatures capable of wonder and worship, who can feel ourselves to be addressed by God in the fullness of his creation" (2014, 81, emphasis in original).[5]

---

[3] Perhaps it is worth recalling here St. Paul's observation that it is in the power of the Spirit that Jesus is raised from the dead (cf. Rom 8:11). We also note that in the baptism of Jesus he is conferred with the descending Spirit, presumably suggesting that it is the Spirit who empowers Jesus for mission. If the Spirit is that central to what Jesus is about, why not apply the same to that dimension of God we call the Father?

[4] And as David Nikkel (2019) illustrates, the spiritual significance of embodiment belongs not merely to Christianity but to all forms of religion.

[5] To which David G. Kirchhoffer adds, "Whereas the tradition has

Embodiment belongs primarily to the cosmic creation, subsequently, to the vast array of embodied creatures that populate our earth, and only laterally to our unique role within the cosmos as earthlings. As earth creatures we are unique, but so are all the other embodied creatures with whom we share the web of life.

Influenced by the growing corpus of multidisciplinary wisdom, the identification of incarnation with bodily unfolding seems to be moving in three significant directions: relational identity, the sensuous body, and transhuman embodiment.

Relational Identity

This is mainly a psychological development, with Israeli/French psychoanalyst Bracha Ettinger (2006) at the forefront. While the patriarchal preoccupation (from Aristotle through Freud) is that of the infant separating from the maternal womb in order to realize an autonomous, individualized identity, Ettinger's "matrixial trans-subjectivity" claims that the growth process in the mother's womb is characterized by a foundational pattern that Ettinger names as "subjectivity-as-encounter." This foundational and enduring pattern means that from our earliest formative moments we are programmed for relationship, not for fierce competition leading to robust individualism. This psychological insight, supported by theorists such as Nancy Chowdrow, Lucy Irigary, and Julia Kristiva (to name but a few), has been adopted by several feminist theologians, notably Grace Jantzen, Carter Heyward, and Lisa Isherwood. For a more detailed overview, see Lyons (2015).[6]

---

usually talked about being *in* the world, the great realization of the latter half of the twentieth century may indeed be that we *are* the world" (quoted in Boeve, De Maeseneer, and Van Stichel, 2014, 185).

[6] I ask the reader's forbearance for frequently revisiting and developing afresh this foundational phenomenon of *relationality*. From my perspective, it is the heart and soul of all reality, human and nonhuman alike, and consequently will be highlighted as the neglected and underrated dimension of incarnation as understood for much of Christian

The Sensuous Body

Christian theology exhibits a long allegiance to the patriarchal anthropology of classical Greek times, inherited mainly through Aristotle.[7] Here the heavy emphasis is on rationality, individualism, and the superiority of the male. Correspondingly, the emotions, senses, subjective human experience, interactive behavior, and the womb formation of the female is not merely subverted, but for much of Christian history, these other dimensions were demonized. Particularly in the psychosexual realm, widespread repression ensued, leading to our contemporary cultural landscape where the outpouring of repressed sexualized energy explodes all around us. The awaited integration is a daunting cultural task, with theology confusedly struggling on how to embrace the whole person, and not merely the rational, ensouled dimension. How then do we revisit and reinterpret our primordial Christian story—the incarnated Jesus—so as to include rather than dismiss all these other God-given dimensions of our incarnational identity? Hopefully, the reflections of the present work go some way to offering an answer to that question.

Transhuman Embodiment

For the multidimensional human body to grow and flourish, it needs the contextualization of the other bodies to which humans belong, especially the earth and cosmic bodies. In the

---

history. Of course, the foundational relationality I am seeking to reclaim in this book extends beyond Christian belief. On the microscopic scale it seems to underpin the world of quantum reality (cf. Rovelli 1996), and on the grand macro level, we see it at work in the religious concept of a Trinitarian God (LaCugna 1991; Fox 2001), equivalents for which are discernible in other world religions (Panikkar 2006).

[7] The patriarchal consciousness/culture alluded to many times in this book predates Aristotle by at least five thousand years. Carol P. Christ (2016) provides a useful overview, clarifying the various uses of the term employed in the present work.

words of quantum physicist Lothar Schafer (2013, 76), "The inner potential in you is cosmic. When you actualize your potential, the cosmic wholeness is actualizing in you. You could say you are an embodiment of cosmic potentiality." Increasingly, spiritual development is viewed as interrelated with the well-being of all the other creatures that share the web of life with us. Today, many more Christians are asking: Why judge the spiritual significance of other embodied life-forms in terms of the human?

Perhaps they have spiritual and theological meaning in their own right (cf. Deane-Drummond 2014; Johnson 2014). Should we not be considering these other embodied forms as divine incarnations as well, particularly the animal dimension of our being and becoming (cf. Haraway 2003; Moore 2014)? After all, God first appeared in the body of the universe and in a vast range of embodied forms long before identifying with humanity.

Today, *incarnation* is a term with multiple meanings, all focused in one way or another around the notion of embodiment. All forms of embodiment—from bacteria to the universe—bear witness to a God who loves bodies and chooses the corporeal form in every initiative of co-creation (more in Nikkel 2019). Everything in creation grows and flourishes in an embodied context. While Spirit represents the energetic life force of everything in creation, clearly the body is the medium through which Spirit-power evolves and flourishes. How do we reconceptualize incarnation to include all forms of embodiment from the cosmos itself to the tiny bacteria, and how do we reenvision the embodiment of Jesus as a fresh and empowering articulation of that vision?

Interreligious Grounding

Global theology, or doing theology in a global context, is an emerging trend of the twenty-first century.[8] The integration of

---

[8] Several publications of recent times support this claim, e.g., Stephen B. Bevans (2009); Darren C. Marks (2017); Gerry L. Martin (2019).

wisdom from disciplines such as science, anthropology, ecology, and economics features in the work of several theologians around the world today. Despite this enlarged, integrated horizon, when it comes to the wisdom of other world religions, we note an unexpected resistance to such integration. Despite the pioneering work in multifaith dialogue and comparative theology by scholars such as Raimundo Panikkar, John Hick, Paul F. Knitter, and Francis X. Clooney, insights from the other great religions are accepted in spiritual and devotional practices but receive minimal attention in theological discourse. Understandings of incarnation are a case in point.

If the coming of God in Jesus belongs to an axial age characterized by the awakening of a new consciousness (an idea initially floated by Karl Jaspers in the twentieth century), then presumably it is axial (i.e., transformative) for all humanity and not just for Christians. Working from this starting point, we readily see that all the major religions articulate the concept of incarnation. It is hard to imagine that we could have overlooked the evidence for so long.

Hinduism, the oldest of today's major religions. has consistently highlighted the importance of *avatars*. Formally describing various appearances of the God Vishnu, Hinduism cherishes the memory of nine outstanding avatars, the earlier versions being partly human, partly animal, suggesting the integration of the human and animal within the larger creation. The better-known figures are those of Rama, Krishna, and the Buddha (the ninth and final avatar).[9]

In all versions of Buddhism, particularly in the Mahayana tradition, *bodhisvattas* hold an honored place. These are humans deemed to have attained the essence of *bodhi* but who renounce entry into nirvana in order to help other beings on the journey. Compassion is considered to be an outstanding virtue of this

---

[9] A tenth, Kalkin, is postulated to appear at the end of the age, to redeem the troubled world and restore harmony.

holy person. While Buddhism does not adopt a notion of divinity comparable to other theistic religions, nonetheless the bodhisvatta characterizes a sense of transcendence made more real and tangible through these incarnation-type figures.

In the Muslim faith, *prophets* are among the most emulated and empowering figures. A large number have been recognized, but eight hold special prominence: Adam, Seth, Enoch, Abraham, Moses, David, and Jesus, with Muhammad as the final prophet, after whom there are no more. The mission of the prophets, variously described as messengers (*rusul*) or ambassadors (*mursulum*), is to call the people to greater fidelity in allegiance to the one God.[10]

Moving beyond the formal religions, we know today of various articulations of the embodied presence of God in the religious beliefs of indigenous peoples. Worthy of note too is the *diviner* in various African religions, and the *shaman* (or *shamanness*) in many prehistoric faiths.

When it comes to the major religions we tend to emphasize differences, while bypassing or undermining significant commonalities. I suggest that the commonalities are far more significant and have not been studied in a way that would liberate deeper truth. Embracing such commonalities would also enhance the work for peace and reconciliation so urgently needed in our violent and divided world. A type of Christian arrogance consistently seems to get in the way. The Christian Jesus, it is argued, is really God and not just a representative of God. Jesus is historically real, whereas many of the other parallels—avatars, bodhisattvas, prophets, diviners, and so on—are mythological or merely symbolic. All these arguments favor differences over commonalities and are often motivated by a subtle, subconscious desire to promote and protect Christian (Western?) imperialism.

---

[10] Similar to the Islamic prophet, and often compared with the Hindu Brahman (holy man), is the notion of the *guru* in Sikhism. There have been ten outstanding gurus, beginning with Guru Nanak, the founder of Sikhism.

Perhaps another fear that fuels the resistance is the perceived relativism in contemporary studies in Christology, particularly as promoted by scholars like Jacques Dupuis, Roger Haight, and Michael Amaladoss, whose understanding of Jesus is strongly influenced by interreligious considerations. Drawing comparative examples from other religions can and does enrich our Christology. The parallel examples cited above—avatars and so forth—are all human creatures (not divine) but considered to be so highly evolved that they serve as models, ideals, or archetypes for humans generally, inviting and challenging us to grow more deeply into our religious faith.

In Christology today, we are moving in a similar direction, highlighting the humanity of Jesus rather than his divinity. Nobody seeks to deny or undermine the divinity of Jesus. Instead, the desire of a growing body of Christians today is to prioritize and internalize more deeply the humanity of Jesus, as the primary exemplar of the human face of God made radically visible on earth. This revelation of God—in and through the humanity of Jesus—has often been undermined and sidelined because of an unhealthy preoccupation with the divinity, considered to be of supreme importance to uphold and safeguard ecclesiastical authority. That same preoccupation with patriarchal power, and its serious unraveling in our time, is foundational to several of the theological shifts being explored in the present work.

Dislodging the Postcolonial Baggage

For almost two thousand years we have adopted a patriarchal backdrop to our understanding of the Christian faith, and the ensuing shape of Christian theology. Most Christians are not even aware of this baggage. Consequently, many of us inhabit an inner space badly damaged by *internalized oppression*. In keeping with the spirit of nonviolent living, as Jesus wishes all Christians to live, we should never collude with our own oppression. Christians have been doing that for centuries.

Postcolonialism is one of several forms of conscientization inviting us to more adult and informed ways of living out our faith today. It draws our attention to the residue to which humans so easily cling on, long after the external colonizers have left our shores. In the case of a major religion, of course, the colonizing forces hung around much longer than many of us suspected. Fortunately, the multidisciplinary research of our time—in disciplines such as postcolonialism—brings a fresh, if disturbing, transparency to our religious landscape, with a range of urgent challenges briefly reviewed herewith.

A critical aspect of this research is the issue of *imperial kingship*. It seems to me that Christian scholars have not dealt well with this substantial background material, with some notable exceptions, specifically that of American Scripture scholar Wes Howard-Brook (2010; 2016). In the time of Jesus, God was understood to be a kinglike figure who reigned in the heavens above and ruled all on earth through a hierarchical set of structures. God's primary role was to rule and re-create a world that had become perverse and evil through human sinfulness.

Such divine governance was assumed to work as good kingly rule on earth operated. The king carefully chose a hierarchical structure mediating down through the different layers of order and discipline. God chose ideal humans to assist in this task, themselves belonging to royal families and therefore always male. In the Hebrew Scriptures, King David tends to be regarded as the outstanding model, despite the fact that much of the research of the twentieth century shows him to have been an extremely violent and reckless ruler.

Despite this well-planned strategy (by the ruling God), things seem to get progressively worse, until eventually the divine king had to send his own beloved Son to be the supreme divine rescuer. At least Mark and Matthew (of the four evangelists) considered him to be a direct descendant of the great King David. At the hands of the Roman forces (with the approval of the Jewish authorities, it seems) he died an ignominious death, which the

Gospel writers interpreted as a kinglike death, with trials and procedures appropriate for a royal victim. For those same evangelists it was a short step to declare the same Jesus the gloriously risen king in the heavenly realm.

Many of the early Christian communities clung to this notion of Jesus as a divine rescuer, but not all of them. Some discerned in the rubric of the kingdom of God (*basileia tou theou*) a countercultural stance, fiercely opposed to royal patronage and prophetically committed to an alternative strategy of mutual empowerment. To this new empowering vision Jesus gave his entire public ministry, to the point where it cost him his life, crucified as a subversive on a Roman cross.

As I indicate in a number of previous works (O'Murchu 2014; 2017), the imperial tenor of this new dispensation is, in itself, a major barrier to accessing its deeper meaning. The English word *kingdom*, from the Greek *basileia,* immediately sets us on a deviant course. Other possible translations based on Hebrew or Aramaic give us more direct access to the original oral tradition. My favorite—despite its clumsy English feel—is the renaming of the kingdom of God as the *Companionship of Empowerment*.[11] Two central values come to the fore here: (1) collaborative empowerment rather than domination from on high, an alternative strategy adopted by Jesus particularly in the parable and miracle narratives; and (2) a strategy of mutual engagement, rather than wisdom from any superior source, as illustrated in the open table fellowship of the Gospels.

It is in the establishment of this new empowering companionship that the incarnation of God in Jesus creates a radical new

---

[11] Originally, I borrowed this phrase from Scripture scholar John Dominic Crossan (1991, 421–22). In more recent times Crossan himself seems to favor another version: the *household of God*. Some commentators view the notion of household at the time of Jesus as a patriarchal structure of domination and control. It strikes me, however, that the notion of household in the New Testament is a great deal more complex than the external patriarchal veneer, as illustrated by Michael Crosby in his understanding of the biblical household (Crosby 2012).

religious paradigm, one so novel and revolutionary that it has taken Christian scholarship some two thousand years to catch up with its revolutionary scope. While some scholars seek to locate this new "kingdom" within the covenantal rule of God in the Hebrew Scriptures, many more consider the New Testament notion of the kingdom as a radical departure not merely from the Hebrew Scriptures but indeed from the divine imperialism discernible in the other great religions as well. Already back in the 1980s, American scholar Thomas Sheehan (1986) claimed that Jesus sought to get rid of all formal religion, desiring instead a creation-based spirituality of love and justice in the name of the new reign of God.

The Companionship of Empowerment marks a major shift in our understanding of Christian incarnation. Contrary to most other embodiments of God recorded in the great religions, this new companionship shifts the focus from God's identity with outstanding individual heroes to empowering communities.[12] The new heroism is in the collaborative endeavor to deliver a profound cultural transformation, not merely for humans but for all creation.[13] A new empowering, communal spirituality is what Jesus wanted, which remains the deep archetypal desire of all Christians to this day.

And we must not restrict our understanding of Christian incarnation—and its unique embodied expression in the Companionship of Empowerment—to merely the past few thousand years. The God who befriends us in our human embodiment has been journeying with us for a long time, an evolutionary trajectory outstripping the mere two-thousand-plus years postulated by Christianity. As a human species, we have known Immanuel—God is

---

[12] We need to note in passing that Trinitarian theology, over recent decades, has been moving in the same direction. See the valuable overview in Johnson (2007).

[13] Almost single-handedly, American scholar Wes Howard-Brook (2016) grounds the New Testament understanding of the kingdom of God in the original creation story of Genesis 1.

with us—for several thousands of years. That Immanuel, however, did not first appear in the historical Jesus of two-thousand-plus years ago; that energizing incarnational presence had been around for billions of years previously.

This alternative empowering vision struggled to survive as most of the deluded people continued to invest their hope in the ancient divine imperialism. And eventually that faith in royal divine power won the day when the Roman emperor Constantine, in the fourth century, earned state (royal) approval for the Christian faith. Then began a long collusion between secular kings and holy kings (popes). Even when they agreed to part company and go their separate ways, they retained a mirror reflection of one another. The church became the great loser, seriously undermining the liberating empowerment of the gospel, and frequently abandoning it entirely.

Of course, there were times when the archetypal truth of the Gospels broke through, and we began to glimpse the deeper vision. We see it particularly in some of the prophetic breakthroughs of the Middle Ages: the rise of the Franciscans, the emergence of the Beguines, the revival of mysticism. Not until the twentieth century, however, did Scripture scholars on a more extensive scale name the serious betrayal of the foundational vision, retrieving once more the empowering alternative for which Christians had often hungered. With lay scholars outpacing clerical ones, the current reform is more likely to endure, despite the fact that several Church structures are still embedded in sanctioned royal power.

Letting Go for Letting Be

Much of this chapter relates to clearing the clutter and rubble that have accumulated over the Christian centuries. Three issues in particular have been identified: a preoccupation with patriarchal power, resulting in an imperial Christology, reinforcing an institutional understanding of Church. Throughout much of Christendom, therefore, there prevailed a power-based ideology rather than an empowering theology. For the people of God generally, that powerful ideology is rapidly losing meaning and credibility, despite the fact that church authorities still cling to it. As we move deeper into the twenty-first century, an empowering theology is likely to gain momentum and cultural significance.

From within this new theological context, incarnation signifies a great deal more than the inherited embodiment in the individual person of Jesus:

- Embodiment is likely to become the single most significant feature. In the new paradigm, the primary embodiment of God in creation is that of the Great Spirit (not Jesus).

- In the energy-creativity of the Great Spirit, all embodied forms—from the cosmos to subatomic particles—illuminate the embodied presence of God in our world.

- Spirit co-creates through bodies, all bodies. Contrary to an earlier negative view of bodies, we must learn to cherish and care for bodies as the Spirit's primary articulation and expression of empowering creativity.

- Evolution celebrates a range of incarnational bodies in creation, from the vast galaxies to the invisible subatomic particles. We humans are among the most recent forms of such incarnational creativity.

- As a human species, our incarnational evolving story has been unfolding over a time span of 7 million years, and the divine presence has been with us throughout that entire time.

- For most of that time—it seems—we lived in a close convivial relationship with the earth body, and we behaved in a way that proved fruitful and creative for ourselves and for the web of life to which we belong. Consequently, we got it right for most of the time.[14] Evidence for being

---

[14] We got it right (in the sense of behaving creatively and respon-

flawed sinful creatures finds little support in our long evolutionary story (more in O'Murchu 2018).

- At a high point in our evolutionary development—the axial epoch of some two thousand years ago—God in Jesus evolves an archetypal incarnational presence to affirm, confirm, and celebrate all we had achieved over the 7 million years.

- This divine affirmation of our incarnational unfolding is based on an empowering vision described in the Gospels as the kingdom of God. To this empowering vision Jesus gave his life—and in the end it cost him his very life. His untimely death has nothing to do with divine rescue. Rather, Jesus models for us—in both life and death—how we must rescue ourselves when we get things badly wrong.

- The incarnational empowerment of Jesus evolves into an embodied expression radically different from the anthropocentric forms of the time. Instead of being modeled on outstanding patriarchal heroes, like the prophets in the Hebrew Scriptures or John the Baptizer in the New Testament, Jesus opted for empowering communities, primarily targeting the marginalized and oppressed.

- The incarnational embodied vision of Jesus is based on what the Greek New Testament names as the kingdom of God—dangerously misleading language, misrepresenting an oral Aramaic medium for which the Companionship of Empowerment would be a more responsible translation.

---

sibly) but not perfect. There is no room for the notion of perfection in an evolutionary universe. Ours is a paradoxical creation flourishing through the dialectical blend of creation-cum-destruction, as outlined in previous sections of this book. If we were at one time a perfect species (before the fall), then we were effectively robots, without freedom or the capacity for creativity. Such embodied creatures would be of no value to the Great Spirit. Our freedom to err—and hopefully learn from our mistakes—is a central feature of our graced, God-given identity.

Toward an Incarnational Church

Throughout the two thousand years of Christendom, the vision and message of Jesus were transmitted through a range of social structures, most of which bear little resemblance to what Jesus was about as the human face of God made radically visible on earth. An ecclesial structure, called the church, gradually assumed responsibility for rescuing deviant humans from this vale of tears. It quickly became the resource that alone could deliver the new freedom, declaring that outside the church there is no salvation. It denounced the material creation and sought to separate humans from the nourishing web of life, thus instigating crippling levels of alienation and disempowerment. And worst of all, it lost sight of the foundational vision of Jesus (embodied also by St. Paul) that was focused on empowering communities.

Inscribed in the soul of the Christian people is a hunger for such empowering communities. It has surfaced several times in Christian history and has consistently been suppressed, sometimes with oppressively violent means (as in the Inquisition of the thirteenth to fourteenth centuries). The most recent upsurge in the ecclesial yearning for authentic community was that of the basic ecclesial communities (BECs) in the closing decades of the twentieth century. Despite its immense inspiration, the movement met with a great deal of ecclesiastical resistance.

The tendency to view such communal developments in a negative light is itself related to the petrified need to protect ecclesiastical power. That, in turn, arose from the neglect—some might say suppression—of what we now understand to be the central vision of Jesus as outlined in the Gospels, namely the kingdom of God, renamed above as the Companionship of Empowerment. Instead of a church ever ready to serve the new companionship and proclaim it as the primary truth of Christian faith, the emerging church after Constantine gradually subverted the empowering vision into submissive patriarchal alliance. Church took priority over kingdom; even to this day many theologians view fidelity to the church as the only authentic way to serve the new reign of God.

The diminishing influence of all churches today is rapidly approaching terminal decline. It is not just about fallout from sexual abuse, the deserting faithful, or a dwindling priesthood. Rather it is the death knell for an institution that has not honored its foundational raison d'être, namely the call to be the servant and herald of the Companionship of Empowerment. In all probability Jesus never intended a clericalized institution as the structure to carry forward his empowering communal vision. What he did desire—and it appears that St. Paul got it right—were small, fluid, flexible empowering communities. In and through such communities the incarnational embodiment of Christ could grow and flourish. Without such communities, the church would always be in crisis to one degree or another.

If the church of the future—and here I have in mind all the Christian denominations—wants to witness more authentically to the incarnational presence of our God in the world, the following scriptural and theological foundations need to be reclaimed afresh:

- For much of Christendom, the church has failed to comply with the mandate so clearly stated in the Beatitudes (Mt 6:33): "Seek first the Kingdom of God and its righteousness." It has given first place to itself and its preoccupation with divine kingly rule mediated through patriarchal, ecclesiastical governance. To become credible and empowering, it must realign its life with the foundational priorities of Jesus and the Gospels.
- Structurally, the institutional dimension must give way to fluid, flexible, creative, and empowering communities, broadly the structure adopted by St. Paul, the operational nature of which we glimpse in Acts 2:44–47; 4:32–37. The enthusiasm around BECs in South America, witnessed particularly in the 1970s and 1980s, presented

the church at large with a refounding moment that was, sadly, ignored and even undermined.

- The suppressed foundational narrative of Mary Magdalene and her companions—and the seminal witness in the early Pauline movement—suggests an experience of church that should always prioritize inclusivity, empowerment from the ground up, and a mystical flavor keeping people ever ready to respond to the ever-fresh call of the Spirit. On this score, theologians have some major efforts to undertake in reworking the ecclesial tradition.

Theological Embodiment

For much of Christian history, the embodiment of faith was perceived to happen in and through the church. How that was to be done became the prerogative of a chosen elite (the clergy), delivering goods to the faithful that the latter could not access. In that process a codependent culture ensued, in which the human body and mind became dualistically split from their God-given, earth-based foundation. The human body became highly problematic, and the earth body even more so. And the clerics proclaimed ever more loudly: escape from this crushing reality is the only solution.

The rehabilitation of the body is probably the single greatest challenge facing theology today. The human body is badly wounded, and religion itself has been a major contributory factor to that state of alienation. The disconnection from the earth body also needs substantial redress. And despite the frequency these days of being reminded that we are stardust, intimately bonded with the universe itself, such sentiments are still largely unknown to the many perverted by dysfunctional religiosity.

Currently, the insipid spiritual vacuum is being filled with a range of spiritual panaceas, some with promising prospects for healing and wholeness, others providing comfort and solace, but failing to connect with the breadth or depth of what empower-

ing embodiment looks like. Hopefully the insights of this chapter
point the seeker in the direction of more authentic pathways. And
in due course we hope that all those who seek and find will also
reconstruct a communal forum (church by whatever name) to
re-create the cosmic, planetary, interpersonal, and ecclesial con-
nections so foundational to the empowering liberation promised
in the name of the Great Spirit.

When Theology Embraces Spirituality

*In my view, the human community and the natural
world will go into the future as a single sacred
community or we will both perish in the desert.*

Thomas Berry

*Christianity moves through history carried by the
impulses of domination and exclusion. It despises
uppity women, no-hellers, contemplatives, queers, and
thinks even less of those people outside Christianity
altogether. But without their witness to the nearness
and tender mercies of Emmanuel, the memory of
Christ is impossibly distorted.*

Wendy Farley

On the opening page of her book *Heart of Flesh*, Sr. Joan Chittister writes, "There is a new question in the Spiritual Life; it is the spirituality of the Spiritual Life itself. Life here, and the way we relate to it, rather than life to come and how we guarantee it for ourselves, has become the spiritual conundrum of our age" (1998, 1). Those words were penned at a time when spirituality was a widely debated topic, with several theorists drawing a distinction between *spirituality* and *religion*. As increasing numbers of people were abandoning religion—at least in terms of church practice—even larger numbers were claiming to be spiritual but not necessarily religious.

Joan Chittister distinguishes between the spiritual life and spirituality, the former describing what traditional Christianity adopted in the hope of attaining salvation in a life hereafter, and the latter highlighting a rediscovery of the sacred in the here and now, along with the ensuing search on how to engage responsibly with that discovery. Beneath both definitions lie two worldviews, which have also had an extensive impact on Christian theology throughout the ages.

The spiritual life adopts a three-tier universe of heaven above, the underworld beneath (including hell), and earth in between; in this configuration, the spiritual life specialized in helping to get one from this world to the heavenly abode often referred to as the next world. Spirituality, on the other hand, adopted a one-world view, the oneness referred to in several mystical traditions, where humans work out their salvation by engaging more authentically as God's co-creators in the collaborative task of bringing about heaven on earth. This is also the worldview integral to the science and cosmology of our time. The three-tier structure no longer makes any sense, scientifically or theologically, despite the fact that the creedal assertions of several Christian denominations seek to uphold it as the only authentic way of understanding our world.

In its traditional sense, the spiritual life was also the bulwark against the fragility of life and the certainty of death. It provided the guarantee that despite all the uncertainties of this world, there awaited us in a life hereafter that which would endure and last forever. The spiritual life therefore was postulated on the assumption that life here is fundamentally flawed, that we can't do much to change it for the better, and therefore it is to be tolerated until we experience the release that comes with death.

Today, we deem this view to be theologically fraudulent and spiritually bankrupt.

Spirituality continues to be a complex subject, articulated through a vast range of perspectives. At one end of the polarized divide are the religionists for whom spirituality is impossible unless solidly based on one or another major world religion; in other words, religion comes first, and spirituality follows. At the other end of the spectrum are those who view spirituality as an endowment of great age preexisting religion by several thousand years, and capable of being embraced with, or without, a grounding in formal religion. I favor the priority of spirituality over religion, and also consider it a foundational resource for an authentic empowering theology of the type being outlined in this book.

Spirituality and Consciousness

Spirituality enjoys a significant revival in our time precisely because it is responding to the awakening consciousness engaging our world today. We have long assumed that consciousness is a dimension of human thought and imagination, beginning and ending with the human mind. Today we view consciousness in a very different light, as something vastly bigger and deeper than a mere human endowment. Already in 1931, physicist Max Planck declared, "I regard consciousness as fundamental. I regard matter as a derivative from consciousness." To which physicist Jude Currivan (2017, 233) adds, "Consciousness is not something we have; it's what we and the whole world are." Currivan also claims that this way of seeing and understanding reality is best described as a spiritual perception (2017, 191).

This more wholesome cosmic view of consciousness is central to quantum mechanics, inseparably connected to the whole of life as Niels Bohr claimed, and reiterated in our time by quantum theorist Paul Levy: "The fact that consciousness is an emergent property of the universe implies, given the underlying wholeness of the universe, that consciousness is one of the intrinsic ingredients of the universe. It is as though the universe is curious about itself, and through its intrinsic sentience, is capable of reflecting upon itself" (2018, 75).

Consciousness is a universal cosmic force that is perhaps best understood as the intelligence (information) that gives shape and direction to that energy that is foundational to all creativity. In chapter 6 I described the energy as the outflow of the Great Spirit's creative potentiality. Consciousness therefore could be understood as the Spirit's wisdom animating and sustaining the Spirit's creativity. Here we encounter an overlapping of foundational concepts: *Spirit, spirituality, energy, consciousness, wisdom.* Metaphysical distinction is irrelevant here. In a quantum universe where everything is entangled, the connectedness and not the clarity of separation is what really matters.

Consciousness permeates everything. It is the foundation for all forms of aliveness within and around us. From it all material and physical form derives its existence and its purpose in the grand scheme of things. It is the wisdom of the Spirit inebriating all potentiality. Spirituality, then, becomes the "religious" wisdom best suited to understanding the operations of consciousness and enabling us humans how best to receive and integrate the influence of consciousness.

While religion seeks to maintain focus on the transcendent God, ruling and governing creation, spirituality seeks to link us more deeply with the conscious creativity of the Great Spirit, immanent in creation rather than transcendent to it. While religion favors the God who created ex nihilo, and seeks to draw all things toward itself, spirituality dwells more integrally with the evolutionary spirit ever luring us into a deeper awareness (consciousness) of the mystery that is our very existence. This is largely a new horizon for theological discernment, with attunement to the Great Spirit at its very core.

People of the Story

One of the difficulties in trying to reconcile spirituality and theology lies in the methodology we adopt. As a formal field of study, theology favors rational discourse on the facts provided by the deposit of faith (i.e., revelation from the Scriptures). For much of the Christian era, those facts, as outlined in the Scriptures, were taken literally. And the ensuing interpretation was heavily influenced by the Western, imperial, patriarchal culture, within the limited time context of the past few thousand years of human existence.

Spirituality, on the other hand, *thrives on story*, the deep ancient narrative of the human fascination around the mystery of our existence. Here the context is deep time, and the discerning horizon is as large as creation itself. Discerning the underlying wisdom of myth and story requires a very different mode of interpretation from that normally involved in theological discourse. The discernment begins not with ourselves in our human condition, but with the cosmic/planetary womb from which we are begotten.

The different methodologies reflect two radically different understandings of the mystery we call God. All formal religions acknowledge an imperial divine ruler, imbued with several anthropocentric projections, a God figure often envisioned in our own image as creatures who seek to dominate and control everything in creation. Jesus tends to be identified with this patriarchal God concept. Spirituality, on the other hand, begins with the Great Spirit, that cosmic insinuation that energizes and empowers every movement within and around us. At one time deeply personal, but also transpersonal (as distinct from impersonal), the Great Spirit is both narrator and narrative of creation's evolving story.

We are the progeny of a storied universe. We are one aspect of a narrative that has been told for eons past. And we are now the privileged participants in that story becoming conscious of its own unfolding. All indications are that we are evolution growing into a new quality of self-awareness, which we call *consciousness* (as described in chapter 7). We are not just another chapter or a specific section of the story; rather the story is embedded in the fabric of our being and becoming. Story, I suggest, is the surest way to resolve the great philosophical search for our true identity.

Today the art of storytelling is itself undergoing a metamorphosis. Mythic story has always relied heavily on the human imagination, which today is enhanced with the multi-imagery repertoire of the technological world of social media. While enlarging the scope of our imaginary constructs, social media can also leave us feeling overwhelmed by the weight and incoherence of all that bombards our senses. The invitation to deeper discernment requires an ever more sensitized, attentive response. And the discernment will also require affiliation with an ever-widening group of people representing the evolving complex wisdom of our age.

Language itself will often fail us; as Jesuit scholar Roger Haight states, "Spirituality provides a testing ground for theological language" (2019, 233n1). The ancient intuition of nonverbal perception and understanding is once more on the ascendency— hence, the ever-growing popularity of meditation and other modalities focused on interiority, mindfulness, silence, and solitude. Indeed, this emphasis on inner process and inner journey often makes religionists suspicious of those exploring the emerging spiritual consciousness of our time.

Changing Worldviews

I opened this chapter highlighting the distinction between the spiritual life and spirituality. Returning to the quotation from Sr. Joan Chittister, I wish to clarify at greater length the two worldviews being highlighted. The spiritual life belongs to the three-tier universe of heaven above, the underworld (including hell) beneath, and the problematic earth in between. The spiritual life served as a permanent reminder that life on earth was deeply unsatisfying, which is how God created it. We were never meant to be at home here. Our one and true home is in heaven, above and outside this earth, and the spiritual life provided the resources to (a) help us live in this world while awaiting deliverance to the life hereafter (in another world), and (b) continually reminding us that our best chance of getting to eternal life was by being faithful in our allegiance to the church.

This three-tier spirituality is visible throughout the entire Christian Bible and also arises in many of the great world religions. St. Paul expected this perverse sinful world to end during his lifetime. In fact, the evangelists (those who wrote the Gospels) give the impression that Jesus concurred with this view. And those who take John's Gospel literally can't fail to notice the frequent references to above and below, the former being the heavenly abode of eternal fulfillment, and the realm below denoting all that is transitory and superficial.

This ambivalence toward the created order comes to the fore in virtually every century of Christianity's two-thousand-year story. Penance, asceticism, and continuous prayer are targeted primarily at preparation for the life hereafter, and the populace is continuously scare-mongered by the God who will come to judge at the end of the age, a petrified rhetoric still cherished by evangelical preachers. The fear of a harsh judgment frequently undermines any hope of coming to terms with a God of unconditional love.

Spirituality moves in a very different direction, adopting a worldview more congruent with modern science and cosmology. The three-tier worldview has been largely replaced by a one-world understanding. Moreover, the emphasis has shifted from something fixed and unchanging to an evolutionary reality forever in the process of becoming.[1] Here, spirituality takes on a whole new meaning:

---

[1] Even the Godhead itself is becoming, as claimed by process theology (A. N. Whitehead 1929; also Catherine Keller 2003, Hyo-Dong Lee 2014, Roland Faber 2017).

- It seeks to honor the creativity of God, at work in the whole creation, and not merely in human life, that understanding of the Holy One described as the Great Spirit (see chapter 6).
- It advocates openness and receptivity to a God who forever seeks to lure all life into greater complexity and deeper becoming.
- It supports a deep sense of trust in what it perceives to be a God of unconditional love.
- Therefore, instead of trying to make it up to God (reparation) for our sins (the spiritual life), spirituality strives to discern how we too must love unconditionally, just as we have been unconditionally loved.
- Spirituality, therefore, moves in the direction of healing and wholeness—for all life-forms, and not merely for humans.
- Instead of being subject to God (in the patriarchal sense), or serving God in some passive way, spirituality adopts the language of collaboration and co-creation.
- In a word, while the spiritual life advocates a process of *escape* (from this vale of tears), spirituality advocates a program of *engagement*, sometimes articulated in the phrase "helping to bring about heaven on earth."

Spirituality Informing Theology

Theology, too, offers a varied response. Theologians tend to view theology as superior to spirituality, particularly those who publicly affiliate with one or another Christian denomination. In the emerging culture of the lay theologian, one detects a more benign attitude toward spirituality. I conclude the present work with a chapter on spirituality, believing that a vibrant spirituality is central to the third paradigm I outline in this book, and that the discernment required to access theological truth seems largely impossible without such a spiritual grounding.

The following are some of the key elements that constitute *spirituality* as employed in the present work.

First of all, theology, as a Christian concept, begins with the deposit of faith, the revelation of God as outlined in the Judeo-Christian Bible. Such theology also claims to draw wisdom and inspiration from the tradition by which theological insight has been passed on over the Christian centuries. The key players in drawing up such dogmatism were a small, elite group of Roman (European) males; well over 90 percent of humanity had no say in the matter. Clearly this position still holds true for our first paradigm (chapter 2) and in modified form for our second paradigm (chapter 3).

For the third paradigm, this understanding of revelation and tradition is far too time-limited and culturally restricted. The primary focus is that of an imperial God, manifest in an imperial Christ, sanctioned and promoted by a largely patriarchal church. Instead, in part two, we begin with God as Spirit revealing the meaning of the divine (and of all life) through the evolution of creation at large. Here, too, is where spirituality begins, *understood as spirit connecting with Spirit*. And the connection is not merely at the human level but implicates in different but related ways with every organism that constitutes the web of life.

Second, in this context, spirituality seeks to honor God as Spirit, the oldest understanding of divine presence discerned by human beings. Often dismissed as paganlike animism, our ancient ancestors discerned a divine presence transcendent and yet immanent throughout the world of their experience. Humans have for long made that discernment through a convivial relationship with the natural world (an intuition largely lost to contemporary humans). By remaining very close to nature, and living convivially with its unfolding rhythms, unknowingly for the greater part, we befriended the Holy One in the co-creative task of evolutionary unfolding.

Third, no one sector of humanity has captured this convivial spirituality as vividly as the First Nations / indigenous peoples.

They have long named the Holy One as the *Great Spirit*, for which they adopt a broadly similar understanding across several modern cultures (outlined in greater length in a previous work, O'Murchu 2011). Of central importance in this indigenous tradition is the fact that the presence and power of the Spirit are discerned first and foremost through the living earth itself.

This understanding should not be identified with either pantheism or panentheism. It is of a very different significance. In the vibrating energy of creation mediated for us earthlings through the Earth itself, we come to know the divine Spirit as the source of all empowering energy bringing into being and sustaining every life-form known in the history of creation. The energy of creation is itself energized by the Great Spirit. With that vibrating energy,[2] every creative urge unfolds, including the ability of the creator (Father) to create, and with Jesus also understood as a Spirit-filled person (see Borg 2015).

Fourth, human beings seem innately programmed for spirit-to-Spirit connection, a foundational hunger in the human spirit for connection with transcendent possibility. If this possibility is hindered, disrupted, or undermined—and this can result from secular or religious forces—then we encounter evidence for negative spirit energy often described as evil. From the Christian viewpoint, the primary agent of incarnational affirmation and empowerment is not Jesus but the living Spirit of God. As indicated earlier in this work, our preoccupation with Jesus and our desire for an exalted Christology are further evidence of the imperial baggage that has seriously undermined the deeper and broader understanding of incarnation, outlined in chapter 9.

---

[2] Consider the natural imagery often associated with the Holy Spirit: "The world's forests are the lungs we breathe with, the ozone layer is the skin that protects; and the earth's lakes and rivers are the veins and arteries that supply us with vital fluids" (Wallace 2002, 147). "The Spirit ensouls the earth as its life-giving breath, and the earth embodies the Spirit's mysterious interanimation of the whole creation" (Wallace 2005, 125).

In theological terms, therefore, the primary incarnation we need to come to terms with is not the Jesus-based one, but that which is grounded in that divine reality we name as the Holy Spirit of God. That is where it all begins. Leonardo Boff goes so far as to suggest that even God begins from that same primordial truth: "God also belongs to the domain of the Spirit; it could not be otherwise" (2015, 60). The hierarchical ladder of Father, Son, and Holy Spirit may not be as theologically sturdy as we have traditionally assumed. Thanks to the increasing and advancing multidisciplinary wisdom of our time, we are retrieving a deeper ancient wisdom that requires us to redefine everything, even our very understanding of God.

Biblical scholar Wes Howard-Brook captures the crucial issue in this observation: "The biblical sense of the human being as earthly soil suffused with God's Spirit was replaced by a Platonic and Stoic sense of the rational mind reining in the animalistic body" (2010, 473). With such Hellenistic influence, we developed a long history of dualistic splitting, leaving us with a fragmentation of Spirit that distorted our view of everything, including our understanding of the divine presence within and around us. There is much that awaits repair, healing, and reintegration.

Toward a More Integrated Spirituality

Integration has long been considered the desired outcome of a meaningful spirituality. In the codependent paradigm, examined in chapter 2, the envisaged integration could only be attained through the salvific power of the death and resurrection of Jesus. That integration could only be fully realized in a life hereafter, in which case our earthly existence is not a process of integration but a waiting time for the true deliverance from suffering and the consequent escape to the heavenly realm of eternal happiness—all made possible by the death and resurrection of Jesus.

In the second paradigm, which I name as the *imperial Judeo-Christian paradigm* (Creation–Israel–Jesus–Church–Eschaton), there is a shift of emphasis from individual plight toward salvation in and through the church, which alone has the wherewithal for an authentic spirituality, with the accompanying resources for growth and integration. However, the integration always awaits a fuller and final realization at the *eschaton*, the eschatological clause assuring us that God will eventually bring all things to an end in a final act of divine deliverance.

As already indicated in this chapter, the evolutionary paradigm marks a significant shift in spirituality, and an ensuing challenge for integration of several new substantial issues. Recalling the outline—Spirit–Energy–Creation–Evolution–Incarnation–Spirituality—we note that it begins with Spirit and ends with spirituality. Spirit encountering Spirit is one of my favorite definitions of spirituality. Beyond the dualistic split of the sacred versus the secular and matter versus spirit is that underlying oneness wherein everything in creation is imbued with Spirit-power. Here the invitation to integration plumbs depths that I suspect only mystics can really comprehend or appreciate.

Mystical feminist writer Beverly Lanzetta invites us into this integral immersion when she writes,

> A spirituality of benevolence avows to the unwavering constancy of the Great Spirit as ever present, neither judging, rejecting, arbitrary, violent, capricious, indifferent or unforgiving. We are made and composed of Divine Love; we know a loving God who does not withdraw. We know a suffering God who bears the arrogance and deafness of our small selves. . . . We honor the female ground of divinity while working to actualize the holiness of the Divine Feminine in our world. . . . We discover that all violation of truth is an aberration of the Great Mystery within us. We thus become excavators of our own truth, digging through the rubble of our anguish, confusion, and missed opportunities for the keys to where and

how the spirit has been repressed or denied. Our life—in
all its wonder and pain—is our teacher. It is through the
process of spiritual awareness, love, and humility that we
discover holiness within. (2018, 119–20)

Such within-ness is not merely a personal sacred depth. It is
transpersonal, across the whole gamut of creation from the quarks
and leptons to the open-ended universe itself. The Spirit knows no
boundaries nor limitations. Is this the divine insistence, described
so elegantly by John D. Caputo?

God is a spirit who calls, a spirit that can happen anywhere and haunts everything insistently. As to the big picture, the large course the Spirit traverses, the large circle it
always cuts, there is no maybe about it; it must be what it
must be. . . . God is an insistence whose existence can only
be found in matter, space, and time. Where else could God
be God? . . . There is grace, grace happens, but it is the
grace of the world. My entire idea is to reclaim religion as
an event of this world, to reclaim religion for the world,
and the world for religion. (2013, 131, 163, 346–47)

The creative energy of the universe is the primary gift of the
empowering Spirit. Evolution is the long, sacred story of the Spirit's
energizing, characterized throughout by both creativity and paradox (as outlined in chapter 5). Creative grace is not about escape
from this side of the eschaton to a utopian paradise hereafter. That
is just one of our several cruel delusions. As coworkers for and with
the Great Spirit, our spiritual integrity is deeply embedded in the
living earth itself. There is no heavenly world beyond, or anywhere
else to which we can escape. We come to terms with this sacred
space or, from there on, we condemn ourselves to mass alienation.

Just as we can no longer discern the meaning of the universe
through a literal rational reading of reality, neither can we appre-

hend the deeper meaning of the mystery within which we exist and flourish. All truth is mystical, metaphorical, and symbolic, primary articulations of the Spirit at work. All creation is a parable, every bit as complex and profound as the parable stories of Jesus in the Gospels. Creativity abounds in what contemporary theologians call *theopoetics*, an articulation of the embracing mystery requiring a quality of discernment that goes beyond every formal religion and beyond all sacred texts.

Theopoetics suggests that instead of trying to develop a "scientific" theory of God, as systematic theology attempts, theologians should instead try to find God through poetic articulations of their lived, embodied experiences. Theopoetics invites theologians to accept reality as a legitimate source of divine revelation and suggests that both the divine and daily experience are mysterious—in fact, ultra-real—and thus irreducible to literalist dogmas or scientific proofs. Revelation from a theopoetic perspective "is an in-coming, a breaking-in upon the world that takes the world by surprise. That is not 'super-natural' but an amplitude of the way the world works. To live in history is to be structurally subject to surprise, to unforeseeability, to the future" (Caputo 2013, 93). Theopoetics suggests that theology can be more akin to poetry than physics. Theopoetics is the art of using words and thoughts that speak to the reader in an aesthetic and existential way, evoking the kind of spiritual awakening described in the present chapter.[3]

---

[3] Theopoetics is a theological process originally developed by Stanley Hopper and David Leroy Miller in the 1960s and furthered significantly by Amos Wilder with his 1976 text, *Theopoetic: Theology and the Religious Imagination*. In recent times there has been a revitalized interest in theopoetics with new work being done by L. Callid Keefe-Perry, Rubem Alves, Catherine Keller, John Caputo, Roland Faber, and others. For useful overviews, see Scott Holland (2007) and Heather Walton (2019).

Conclusion

More than anything else, this new evolutionary spirituality invites us to transcend and outgrow several forms of inherited reductionism. We have been indoctrinated in keeping things small and manageable; it feeds into our patriarchal addiction for domination and control. It subverts the mystery and undermines the organic oneness that characterizes Spirit-power. We are beneficiaries of a divine hospitality that has been eluding us for the patriarchal era of the past eight thousand to ten thousand years (the postagricultural era). Hospitality is not just about humans and our ways of engaging each other. The abundant proclivity of the universe and planet Earth is the foundational hospitality (acknowledging the highly destructive forces that are integral to such abundance). All is gift, and we need to come to terms with that prodigious truth; otherwise we are setting ourselves on a sure road to perdition.

Such hospitality brings us full circle. The hospitable earth is itself a place of welcoming shelter, home to the Great Spirit, whose creative energy exudes through every being. This is where theology needs to begin, not with some transcendent patriarchal deity but with the living energizing Spirit whose empowering grace is mediated for us earthlings, through the earth itself. When the theologians honor the starting point of Spirit-connecting-with-Spirit (spirituality), then they will employ a very different methodology—not so much based on rational metaphysics and a more literal reliance on the scriptural deposit of faith—but based primarily on a mystical organic connection with the Spirit-filled energy of creation itself.

Theology then becomes a contemplative, collaborative endeavor in which all humans become potential participators. The mystery of the human and the sacredness of earth belong to the one organic web. In the realm of the Spirit, all is One.

Bibliography

Abram, David. 1996. *The Spell of the Sensuous*. New York: Random House.

———. 2010. *Becoming Animal: An Earthly Cosmology*. New York: Vintage Books.

Armstrong, Karen. 1996. *In The Beginning*. London: Vintage.

Bauman, Whitney. 2005. "Creatio ex Nihilo, Terra Nullis, and the Erasure of Presence," in Catherine Keller and Laurel Kearns, eds., *EcoSpirit: Religions and Philosophies for the Earth*, 353–72. New York: Fordham University Press.

———. 2014. *Religion and Ecology: Developing a Planetary Ethic*. New York: Columbia University Press.

Bevans, Stephen B. 2009. *An Introduction to Theology in Global Perspective*. Maryknoll, NY: Orbis Books.

Bermejo-Rubio, Fernando. 2014. "Jesus and the Anti-Roman Resistance." *Journal for the Study of the Historical Jesus* 12, nos. 1–2: 1–105.

Boehm, Christopher. 1999. *Hierarchy in the Forest: The Evolution of Egalitarian Behavior*. Cambridge, MA: Harvard University Press.

———. 2012. *Moral Origins*. New York: Basic Books.

Boeve, Liven, Yves De Maeseneer, and Ellen Van Stichel. 2014. *Questioning the Human: Toward a Theological Anthropology for the Twenty-First Century*. New York: Fordham University Press.

Boff, Leonardo. 2013. *Christianity in a Nutshell*. Maryknoll, NY:
     Orbis Books.
———. 2015. *Come Holy Spirit*. Maryknoll, NY: Orbis Books.
Borg, Marcus. 2015. *Jesus: The Life, Teachings, and Relevance of
     a Religious Revolutionary*. New York: Harper One.
Bourgeault, Cynthia. 2008. *The Wisdom Jesus*. Boston: Shamb-
     hala Publications.
———. 2010. *The Meaning of Mary Magdalene*. Boston: Shamb-
     hala Publications.
———. 2014. *The Holy Trinity and the Law of Three*. Boulder,
     CO: Shambhala Publications.
Bowles, Samuel, and Herbert Gintis. 2013. *A Cooperative Species*.
     Princeton, NJ: Princeton University Press.
Bracken, Joseph. 2014. *The World in the Trinity: Open-Ended Sys-
     tems in Science and Religion*. Minneapolis: Fortress Press.
Brandon, S. G. F. 1967. *Jesus and the Zealots*. New York: Charles
     Scribner and Sons.
Brock, Rita N., and Rebecca Ann Parker. 2008. *Saving Paradise*.
     Boston: Beacon Press.
Brooten, Bernadette. 1982. *Women Leaders in the Ancient Syna-
     gogue*. Chico, CA: Scholars Press.
Brueggemann, Walter. 1986. *The Hopeful Imagination*. Minne-
     apolis: Fortress Press.
———. 2005. *The Book That Breathes New Life*. Minneapolis:
     Augsburg Fortress.
Bruni, Lungino. 2008. *Reciprocity, Altruism, and Civil Society*.
     New York: Routledge.
Cannato, Judy. 2006. *Radical Amazement*. Notre Dame, IN: Sorin
     Books.
Caputo, John D. 2013. *The Insistence of God*. Bloomington: Indi-
     ana University Press.
Carroll, James. 2014. *Christ Actually*. New York: Viking.
Cavanaugh, William T. 2016. *Being Consumed: Economics and
     Christian Desire*. Grand Rapids: Eerdmans.
Chittister, Joan. 1998. *Heart of Flesh*. Grand Rapids: Eerdmans.
Chopra, Deepak. 1989. *Quantum Healing*. New York: Bantam Books.

Christ, Carol P. 2016. "A New Definition of Patriarchy: Control of Women's Sexuality, Private Property, and War." *Feminist Theology* 24: 214–25.

Christian, David. 2004. *Maps of Time: An Introduction to Big History*. Berkeley: University of California Press.

Christie, Douglas. 2013. *The Blue Sapphire of the Mind*. New York: Oxford University Press.

Clayton, Philip. 2008. *Adventures in the Spirit*. Minneapolis: Fortress Press.

Clooney, Francis Xavier. 2010. *Comparative Theology*. London: Wiley-Blackwell.

Corley, Kathleen. 2002. *Women and the Historical Jesus*. Santa Rosa, CA: Polebridge Press.

———. 2010. *Maranatha: Women's Funerary Rituals and Christian Origins*. Minneapolis: Fortress Press.

Crosby, Michael. 2012. *Repair My House*. Maryknoll, NY: Orbis Books.

Crossan, John Dominic. 1991. *Religious Worlds: Primary Readings in Comparative Perspective*. Kendall Hunt Publishing: Dubuque, IA.

———. 1996. *Who Is Jesus?* San Francisco: HarperSanFrancisco.

———. 2010. *The Greatest Prayer*. New York: HarperCollins.

Currivan, Jude. 2017. *The Cosmic Hologram*. Rochester, VT: Inner Traditions.

David, J. R. 2013. *Internalized Oppression: The Psychology of Marginalized Groups*. New York: Springer.

Davidson, John. 2004. *The Secret of the Creative Vacuum*. New York: Random House.

Davies, Oliver. 2014. "Neuroscience, Self and Jesus Christ," in Boeve et al. (2014), 79–100.

Deane-Drummond, Celia. 2009. *Christ and Evolution*. Minneapolis: Fortress Press.

———. 2014. *The Wisdom of the Liminal: Evolution and Other Animals in Human Becoming*. Grand Rapids: Eerdmans.

———. 2017. *A Primer in Ecotheology*. Eugene, OR: Cascade Books.

Delio, Ilia. 2008. *Christ in Evolution*. Maryknoll, NY: Orbis Books.

———. 2013. *The Unbearable Wholeness of Being*. Maryknoll, NY: Orbis Books.

———. 2015. *Making All Things New*. Maryknoll, NY: Orbis Books.

De Waal, Frans. 2010. *The Age of Empathy*. New York: Random House.

Dürr, Hans-Peter. 2010. *Geist, Kosmos, und Physic*. Amerang (Germany): Crotona Verlag GmbH.

Edwards, Denis. 2019. *Deep Incarnation*. Maryknoll, NY: Orbis Books.

Ehrlich, Paul R. and Peter H. Raven. 1964. "Butterflies and Plants: A Study in Coevolution." *Evolution*. 18(4): 586-608.

Eisenstein, Charles. 2011. *Sacred Economics*. Berkeley, CA: Evolver Editions.

Eldredge, Niles. 1985. *Time Frames*. New York: Simon and Schuster.

Ettinger, Bracha. 2006. *The Matrixial Borderspace*. Minneapolis: University of Minnesota Press.

Faber, Roland. 2004. *God as Poet of the World*. Louisville, KY: Westminster John Knox Press.

———. 2017. *The Becoming of God*. Eugene, OR: Cascade Books.

Farley, Margaret A. 2006. *Just Love: A Framework for Christian Sexual Ethics*. New York: Continuum.

Fox, Everett. 1983. *The Five Books of Moses*. New York: Schocken.

Fox, Patricia. 2001. *God as Communion*. Collegeville, MN: Liturgical Press.

Goodwin, Brian. 1994. *How the Leopard Changed Its Spots: The Evolution of Complexity*. New York: Charles Scribner.

Green, Brian. 2000. *The Elegant Universe*. London (UK): Random House.

Greenstein, George. 1988. *The Symbiotic Universe*. New York: William Morrow.

Gregersen, Niels. 2015. *Incarnation: On the Scope and Depth of Christology*. Minneapolis: Fortress Press.

Haight, Roger. 2019. *Faith and Evolution*. Maryknoll, NY: Orbis Books.

Haraway, Donna J. 2003. *The Companion Species Manifesto: Dogs, People and Significant Otherness*. Chicago: Pickly Paradigm.

Haughey, John C. 2015. *A Biography of the Spirit*. Maryknoll, NY: Orbis Books.

Haught, John F. 2003. *Deeper Than Darwin*. Boulder, CO: Westview Press.

———. 2010. *Making Sense of Evolution*. Louisville, KY: Westminster John Knox Press.

———. 2015. *Resting on the Future*. New York: Bloomsbury.

Hodgson, Peter C. 1994. *Winds of the Spirit*. London: SCM Press.

Holland, Scott. 2007. "Theology Is a Kind of Writing: The Emergence of Theopoetics." *CrossCurrents* 1: 317–31.

Howard-Brook, Wes. 2010. *Come Out My People!* Maryknoll, NY: Orbis Books.

———. 2016. *Empire Baptized: How the Church Embraced What Jesus Rejected*. Maryknoll, NY: Orbis Books.

Hrdy, Sarah Blaffer. 2009. *Mothers and Others: The Evolutionary Origins of Mutual Understanding*. Cambridge, MA: Cambridge University Press.

Johnson, Elizabeth A. 2003. *Truly Our Sister*. New York: Continuum.

———. 2007. *Quest for the Living God: Mapping Frontiers in the Theology of God*. New York: Bloomsbury.

———. 2014. *Ask the Beasts! Darwin and the God of Love*. New York: Bloomsbury.

———. 2018. *Creation and the Cross*. Maryknoll, NY: Orbis Books.

Johnson, Kurt, and David Robert Ord. 2012. *The Coming Inter-Spiritual Age*. Vancouver: Namaste Publications.

Kamitsuka, Margaret D., ed. 2010. *The Embrace of Eros*. Minneapolis: Fortress Press.

Kaufman, Gordon. 2004. *In the Beginning . . . Creativity*. Minneapolis: Fortress Press.

Keller, Catherine. 2003. *Face of the Deep*. New York: Routledge.

Kim, Grace Ji-Sun. 2011. *The Holy Spirit, Chi, and the Other*. New York: Palgrave Macmillan.

King, Moray B. 2001. *Quest for Zero Point Energy*. Kempton, IL:
    Adventures Unlimited Press.
Kolbert, Elizabeth. 2014. *The Sixth Extinction: An Unnatural History*. London: Bloomsbury.
Kübler-Ross, Elisabeth. 1969. *On Death and Dying*. New York:
    Methuen.
LaCugna, Catherine. 1991. *God for Us: The Trinity and Christian Life*. New York: Harper.
Lanzetta, Beverly. 2018. *The Monk Within*. Sebatopol, CA: Blue
    Sapphire Books.
Lasch, Christopher. 1979. *The Culture of Narcissism: American Life in an Age of Diminishing Expectations*. New York:
    W. W. Norton.
László, Erwin. 1998. *The Whispering Pond*. Rockport, MA: Element Books.
———. 2004. *Science and the Akashic Field*. Rochester, VT: Inner
    Traditions.
Leakey, Richard, and Roger Lewin. 1995. *The Sixth Extinction: Patterns of Life and the Future of Humankind*. London:
    Weidenfeld and Nicolson.
Lee, Hyo-Dong. 2014. *Spirit, Qi, and the Multitude*. New York:
    Fordham University Press.
Levy, Paul. 2018. *The Quantum Revelation*. New York: Select Books.
Lindenfors, Patrik. 2017. *For Whose Benefit? The Biological and Cultural Evolution of Human Cooperation*. Springer.
Lyons, Kathleen. 2015. *Mysticism and Narcissism*. Newcastle
    upon Tyne, UK: Cambridge Scholars.
MacKenzie, Catriona, and Natalie Stoljar. 2000. *Relational Autonomy*. New York: Oxford University Press.
Maehle, Gregor. 2012. *Pranayama: The Breath of Yoga*. New
    Delhi: Kaivalya Publications.
Maiter, Sarah, Laura Simich, Nora Jacobson, and Julie Wise.
    2008. "Reciprocity: An Ethic for Community-Based Participatory Action Research." *Action Research* 6: 305–25.
Malone, Mary. 2014. *The Elephant in the Church*. Dublin:
    Columba Press.

Margulis, Lynn. 1998. *The Symbiotic Planet*. New York: Basic Books.

Margulis, Lynn, and Dorian Sagan. 1997. *Slanted Truths: Essays on Gaia, Symbiosis and Evolution*. New York: Springer-Verlag.

Marks, Darren C. 2017. *Shaping a Global Theological Mind*. New York: Routledge.

Martin, Jerry L. 2019. *Theology without Walls*. New York: Routledge.

McCaul, T. 2007. *Yoga as Medicine*. New York: Bantam Books.

McFarland, Ian. 2010. *In Adam's Fall*. New York: Wiley-Blackwell.

Moltmann, Jürgen. 1985. *God in Creation*. New York: Harper and Row.

Moore, Stephen D. 2014. *Divinanimality: Animal Theory, Creaturely Theology*. New York: Fordham University Press.

Moore, Thomas. 1998. *The Soul of Sex*. New York: HarperCollins.

Neusner, Jacob and Bruce Chilton. 2008. *The Golden Rule: The Ethics of Reciprocity in World Religions*. London: Bloomsbury.

Nikkel, David. 2019. *Radical Embodiment*. Eugene, OR: Wipf and Stock.

Oliver, Tom. 2020. *The Self Delusion*. London: Weidenfeld and Nicolson.

O'Murchu, Diarmuid. 2002. *Evolutionary Faith*. Maryknoll, NY: Orbis Books.

———. 2008. *Ancestral Grace*. Maryknoll, NY: Orbis Books.

———. 2011. *In the Beginning Was the Spirit*. Maryknoll, NY: Orbis Books.

———. 2014. *On Being a Postcolonial Christian*. North Charleston, SC: CreateSpace.

———. 2015. *Inclusivity: A Gospel Mandate*. Maryknoll, NY: Orbis.

———. 2017. *Incarnation: A New Evolutionary Threshold*. Maryknoll, NY: Orbis Books.

———. 2018. *Beyond Original Sin*. Maryknoll, NY: Orbis Books.

———. 2019. *When the Disciple Comes of Age*. Maryknoll, NY: Orbis Books.

Orobator, Agbonkhianmeghe. 2018. *Religion and Faith in Africa*. Maryknoll, NY: Orbis Books.

Panikkar, Raimon. 2006. *The Experience of God*. Minneapolis: Fortress Press.

Parkinson, Lorraine. 2015. *Made on Earth: How Gospel Writers Created the Christ*. Richmond, Victoria (Australia): Spectrum Publications.

Patterson, Stephen J. 2014. *The Lost Way*. New York: HarperOne.

Pereira, Ryan Terrence, Carmel M. Malone, and Gerard T. Flaherty. 2018. "Aesthetic Journeys: A Review of Cosmetic Surgery Tourism." *Journal of Travel Medicine* 25, no. 1: 1–8.

Phipps, Carter. 2012. *Evolutionaries*. New York: Harper.

Prigogine, Ilya and Isabelle Stengers. 1984. *Order Out of Chaos: Man's New Dialogue with Nature*. London: William Heinemann Ltd.

Pryor, Adam, and Devan Stahl, eds. 2018. *The Body and Ultimate Concern: Reflections on an Embodied Theology of Paul Tillich*. Macon, GA: Mercer University Press.

Rahner, Karl. 1978. *Foundations of Christian Faith*. New York: Crossroad.

Ridley, Matt. 1996. *The Origins of Virtue: Human Instincts and the Evolution of Cooperation*. London: Penguin.

Rifkin, Jeremy. 2009. *The Empathic Civilization*. Cambridge: Polity Press.

Robinette, Brian D. 2011. "The Difference Nothing Makes: *Creatio ex nihilo*, Resurrection, and Divine Gravity." *Theological Studies* 72, no. 3: 525–57.

Rohr, Richard. 2019. *The Universal Christ*. New York: Convergent.

Rolston, Holmes, III. 1999. *Genes, Genesis, and God*. Cambridge, MA: Cambridge University Press.

Rovelli, C. 1996. "Relational Quantum Mechanics." *International Journal of Theoretical Physics* 35: 1637–78.

Schaberg, Jane. 1987. *The Illegitimate Jesus*. San Francisco: Harper and Row.

Schafer, Lothar. 2013. *Infinite Potential: What Quantum Physics Reveals*. New York: Random House.

Service, Steven R. 2015. *The Lost and Forgotten Gospel of the Kingdom*. Morrisville, NC: Lulu.com.

Seung, Sebastian. 2012. *Connectome: How the Brain's Wiring Makes Us Who We Are*. New York: Houghton Mifflin Harcourt.

Sheehan, Thomas. 1986. *The First Coming: How the Kingdom of God Became Christianity*. New York: Random House.

Shults, F. LeRon, and Jan-Olav Henriksen. 2011. *Saving Desire: The Seduction of Christian Theology*. Grand Rapids: Eerdmans.

Smith, Cyprian. 1987. *The Way of Paradox*. London: Darton, Longman and Todd.

Southgate, Christopher. 2008. *The Groaning of Creation: God, Evolution, and the Problem of Evil*. Louisville, KY: Westminster John Knox Press.

Spong, John Shelby. 1998. *Why Christianity Must Change or Die*. New York: HarperOne.

———. 2016. *Biblical Literalism: A Gentile Heresy*. New York: HarperOne.

Stanley, Christopher D., ed. 2011. *The Colonized Apostle*. Minneapolis: Fortress Press.

Stewart, John. 2000. *Evolution's Arrow*. Canberra: Chapman Press.

Swimme, Brian. 1996. *The Hidden Heart of the Cosmos*. Maryknoll, NY: Orbis Books.

Swimme, Brian, and Thomas Berry. 1992. *The Universe Story*. New York: Penguin.

Swimme, Brian, and Mary Evelyn Tucker. 2011. *Journey of the Universe*. New Haven, CT: Yale University Press.

Tan, Jonathan Y., and Anh Q. Tran. 2016. *World Christianity: Perspectives and Insights*. Maryknoll, NY: Orbis Books.

Taylor, Steve. 2005. *The Fall*. Winchester (UK): O Books.

Teilhard de Chardin, Pierre. 1955. *The Phenomenon of Man*. London: William Collins.

Tickerhoof, Bernard. 2002. *Paradox: The Spiritual Path to Transformation*. New London, CT: Twenty-Third Publications.

Tracy, David. 1994. "The Return of God in Contemporary Theology." *Concilium* 6: 37–47.

Van Lommel. Pim. 2010. *Consciousness before Life*. New York: HarperCollins.

Wallace, Mark I. 2002. *Fragments of the Spirit*. Harrisburg, PA: Trinity Press International.

———. 2005. *Finding God in the Singing River*. Minneapolis: Fortress Press.

Walton, Heather. 2019. "A Theopoetics of Practice: Re-Forming in Practical Theology," *International Journal of Practical Theology* 23: 3–23.

Ware, James P. 2019. *Paul's Theology in Context*. Grand Rapids: Eerdmans.

Whitehead, A. N. 1929. *Process and Reality*. New York: Macmillan.

Wiley, Tatha. 2002. *Original Sin*. New York: Paulist Press.

Williams, Patricia. 2001. *Doing without Adam and Eve*. Minneapolis: Fortress Press.

Winter, Miriam Therese. 2009. *Paradoxology: Spirituality in a Quantum Universe*. Maryknoll, NY: Orbis Books.

Wright, N. T. 2003. *The Resurrection of the Son of God*. London: SPCK.

———. 2013. *Paul and the Faithfulness of God*, Parts I and II. Minneapolis: Fortress Press.

Yong, Amos. 2005. *The Spirit Poured Out on All Flesh*. Grand Rapids: Baker Academic.

Index

Abraham, 47, 175
Abram, David, 121, 167
Adam
  Adam and Eve, 45, 106
  Christ as the new Adam, 30, 33
  Islam, Adam as a prophet in,
    175
  sin of, 14, 24–25, 34
Adams, James Rowe, 60
Age of Empathy (de Waal), 133
akashic field, 109–10
Amaladoss, Michael, 176
Ambrose, Saint, 24
Anselm of Canterbury, 4, 6
Aristotle
  on females as misbegotten
    males, 8, 134, 137
  the human, extolling, 120, 133
  human sexuality, equating to
    biological reproduction, 136
  male role model provided by,
    allegiance to, 135
  patriarchal anthropology of,
    52, 96, 156, 171, 172
  Scholasticism, influence on, 16
Armstrong, Karen, 45, 64
Assmann, Jan, 89
atonement theory, 24, 31, 38–39,
  94, 96
Augustine, Saint, 1, 24, 136
avatars, 174, 175, 176

basic ecclesial communities
  (BECS), 50, 57–58, 95, 129,
  183–84
Bauman, Whitney, 45, 102

Beguines, 51, 56, 180
Berry, Thomas, 80
birthing God metaphor, 123–25
bodhisattvas, compassion of,
  174–75
Boehm, Christopher, 132, 133
Boff, Leonardo, 103, 121, 197
Bohr, Niels, 189
Boniface VIII, Pope, 56
Bourgeault, Cynthia, 33–34, 88,
  158
Bowles, Samuel, 133
Brock, Rita N., 37–38
Brown, Raymond, 5
Brueggemann, Walter, 89–90, 97
Buddhism, 146, 174–75

Caputo, John, 161, 199
Cavanaugh, William, 86
Center for Applied Research in
  the Apostolate (CARA), 67
Chittister, Joan, 187–88, 192
Chopra, Deepak, 112
Christian, David, 101
Christie, Douglas, 70
Church Fathers, 4
Clayton, Philip, 107
Clement V, Pope, 56
clerical sex abuse, 135–36
Clooney, Francis X., 7, 174
co-creation concept, 10–11, 130,
  166–67, 173, 194
Code of Canon Law, 55
codependency
  codependent culture of the
    church, 53, 84, 185

codependency *(continued)*
  codependent paradigm,
    27–28, 197
  codependent spirituality, 39,
    54
  psychological codependency,
    9
co-evolution, 133, 144–45, 150
Companionship of Empower-
    ment, 178–79, 182, 183–84
Connectome (Seung), 154
Constantine, Emperor, 7, 50, 180,
    183
Cooperative Species (Gintis), 133
Copernicus, Nicolaus, 66
Corley, Kathleen, 39, 89
cosmetic surgery, 131–32
Council of Trent, 2, 51–52, 55,
    64–65, 66, 137
Council of Vienne, 56
covenant, 11, 33, 45, 47, 48, 179
Creation-Fall-Redemption
    paradigm, 23, 29, 30, 41, 43
Creation-Israel-Jesus-Church-
    Eschaton paradigm, 43,
    197–98
creative vacuum, 105, 108–12,
    114–15, 120, 139
Crossan, John Dominic, 35, 36,
    58, 64, 129–30
Culture of Narcissism (Lasch),
    131
cupped-hands reflection, 110–11
Currivan, Jude, 116, 152, 189

Daly, Gabriel, 83
Darwin, Charles, 13
Darwinianism, 96, 142, 147,
    149, 153–54, 155
David, King, 47, 101, 175, 177
Davidson, John, 113, 117
Davies, Oliver, 170

de Waal, Frans, 133
Deane-Drummond, Celia, 164,
    173
deep incarnation, 164–68
Deep Incarnation (Edwards), 164
Delio, Ilia, 143
devotionalism, 53–54
Divino Afflante Spiritu document,
    5
dramatic theory, 31
Dupuis, Jacques, 176
Dürr, Hans-Peter, 107

Edwards, Denis, 121, 164–65
Ehrlich, Paul R., 144
Einstein, Albert, 106–107, 114
Eisenstein, Charles, 79–80
Eldredge, Niles, 96
Ely, Richard, 86
embodiment
  the body and, 120–23
  in Companionship of
    Empowerment, 179
  divine intent, embodied
    structure as enriching,
    139–40
  embodied birthing, 120, 130,
    141
  of the Great Spirit, 167, 168,
    181
  healing the wounded body,
    130–35
  incarnation of Christ, 166, 182,
    184
  indigenous peoples, religious
    beliefs on, 175
  Jesus as divine embodiment,
    126, 127, 128–29, 152, 160,
    165
  process of, 170–71
  theological embodiment,
    185–86

transhuman embodiment,
    172–73
The Empathic Civilization
    (Rifkin), 133
end times, 58, 193
entanglement theory, 12, 147,
    190
eschatology, 57–58, 146
eschaton, 57, 198, 199
Ettinger, Bracha, 171
evolutionary imperative
    broad discernment of, 161
    as a co-evolutionary process,
        143–44
    communal obedience, role in, 97
    embodiment, understanding
        through, 129, 140
    overview, 13–15
    purification process, 98
    sensitivity and responsiveness
        to, 130
    sexuality, changing outlook on,
        137
    as a twenty-first century
        development, 7
evolutionary paradigm, 70–71, 198
ex profundis concept, 46, 102,
    106, 117, 119
ex-nihilo creation
    control and mastery, as
        offering, 105
    ex-profundis creation, *vs.*, 46,
        102, 117
    God as above and outside,
        denoting, 123
    imperial governance as
        resulting from, 139
    as patriarchal, 45, 100, 120
    quagmire of the concept, 24
    religion as favoring the
        concept of, 190
    re-visioning, need for, 160

as a widely held view,
    101–102

Faber, Roland, 17, 103
Farley, Margaret A., 122
fecund emptiness, 111, 112
Flaherty, Gerald T., 131
Francis, Pope, 9–10

Gaia theory, 167
genetic mutations, 142–43
Gintis, Herbert, 133
Girard, René, 156
Goodall, Jane, 154
Goodwin, Brian, 154–55
Gould, Stephen J., 147
Great Birther metaphor, 19, 120,
    123, 125
Great Spirit
    as central feature of deep
        incarnation, 168
    as co-creating through bodies,
        167–68, 181
    constancy of as unwavering, 198
    creative grace of, 199
    curiosity of the human mind,
        as awakening, 114
    earth as the home of, 196, 201
    ex profundis as method of
        creation, 46
    foundational creativity of, 103
    as the grace of God, 152
    as immanent in creation, 190
    indigenous peoples experience
        of, 104, 159–60
    liberation promised in the
        name of, 186
    one-world understanding of, 194
    as primordial creative energy,
        102, 117, 122, 123, 141, 167
    transpersonal nature of, 19,
        102, 116, 191

Greenstein, George, 158

Haeckel, Ernst, 20
Haight, Roger, 15, 64, 142, 169, 176, 192
Haught, John F., 147
Heart of Flesh (Chittister), 187
Henriksen, Jan-Olav, 166
heresy, 54–56
Hierarchy in the Forest (Boehm), 132
Higgs, Peter, 108
Higgs field, 108–109
Hinduism, 109–10, 146, 174
Hodgson, Peter, 112, 124
Holy Spirit
    as the breath of God, 45–46
    Clayton, insights on, 107
    creative energy of, 170
    as *energeia*, 112
    as enlivening all that exists, 148
    foundational role of, 108
    Shekenai, identifying with, 106
    Spirit-Power, 115
    as theological focus, 147, 148
    in Trinitarian hierarchy, 94, 158, 165, 197
    as underlying divine empowerment, 95, 110
    See also Great Spirit
How the Leopard Changed Its Spots (Goodwin), 154
Howard-Brook, Wes, 45, 49, 102, 177, 197
Hrdy, Sarah Blaffer, 124, 132–33
Humanae Vitae papal document, 137

imago dei (image of God), 134
imperial Judeo-Christian paradigm, 43, 197–98
infallibility of the pope, 4

internalized oppression, 8, 9, 42, 54, 176
Islam, 14, 47, 146, 175
Israel, 44, 46–49, 197–98

Jansenism, 53
Jaspers, Karl, 174
Jerome, Saint, 4
Jesus Christ
    as an archetypal ancestral figure, 19, 182
    birth of, 125–28
    Christology, 49, 51, 151–52, 168, 176, 180, 196
    collaboration with God, 130
    Constantine as betraying the message of, 50–51, 183
    covenant, understanding Jesus through, 11
    death of, 36–37, 79, 81, 83, 88–89
    deep incarnation of, 164–65, 168
    as divine rescuer, 34–35, 94, 177–78
    embodiment of, re-envisioning, 173
    evolutionary imperative for incarnation of, 129
    Immanuel as beyond the historical Jesus, 180
    the imperial Christ, 16, 95, 97, 177
    Israel and, 48–49
    Jesus and the Christ, distinguishing between, 18
    Kingdom of God as mission of, 74, 184
    mainline view on, 156
    as Messiah, 20, 31, 32, 35
    as the new Adam, 33
    PC stance regarding, 62, 68, 69

as a prophet, 175
redemptive myth of, 14–15
re-envisioning the meaning of, 160–61
resurrection of, 40, 41, 84, 87, 89–91, 98, 197
rural Galilee, holding meetings in, 57
as Savior, 2, 23, 25, 149
shift in theological placement, 160, 163–64, 181, 196
suffering of, 38
John the Baptist, 128–29, 182
Johnson, Elizabeth, 88, 92, 121, 127, 164
Judaism, 32, 43, 46, 47, 146, 152
Jus Novissimum (newest law), 55

Keller, Catherine, 45, 46, 117, 119
King, David, x, 177
Kingdom of God. *See* Companionship of Empowerment
Kolbert, Elizabeth, 85
Kübler-Ross, Elisabeth, 79

Lanzetta, Beverly, 198
Lasch, Christopher, 131
László, Ervin, 109
Laudato Si' papal encyclical, 9–10
Leakey, Richard, 84–85
Levy, Paul, 12, 116, 189–90
Lewin, Roger, 84–85
LGBTIQ movement, 138
Lommel, Pim van, 110, 116
Lucifer, 25–26, 27

magisterium, 3, 5
Malone, Carmel M., 131
Malone, Mary, 90–91
Margulis, Lynn, 153–54

Martin, Jerry L., 7
Mary Magdalene, 87–88, 90, 185
matrixial trans-subjectivity claims, 171
McFague, Sallie, 121, 168
Meister Eckhart, 123
Memra (Word), 105–106
Mendel, Gregor, 142–43
Merleau-Ponty, Maurice, 121
Michael the Archangel, 25–26
Moore, Thomas, 136
moral influence theory, 31
Moral Origins (Boehm), 133
M-theory, 113–14
multiverse, 10, 74, 105. 122

natural selection, 141
the new biology, 154
the new cosmology, 10–11, 78, 94
the new morality, 139
noncontradiction principle, 106

Oliver, Tom, 148
Order Out of Chaos (Prigogine/ Stengers), 153
original sin, 22, 24, 26, 53, 64, 86, 151
The Origins of Virtue (Ridley), 133
Orobator, Agbonkhianmeghe, 67

panentheism, 19, 107, 118, 196
pantheism, 19, 118, 196
paradox
    destruction as a fundamental paradox, 10
    evolution as paradoxical, 118
    flaw, paradox confused with, 85, 149
    as foundation for freedom and creativity, 150
    the great paradox, 17

paradox *(continued)*
  inversion of values as full of,
    136
  paradoxical empowerment,
    89–90
  paradoxical imperative, 80–84
Parker, Rebecca Ann, 37–38
parthenos (virgin), 127–28
Passion of the Christ (film), 36, 38
pathos, suppression of, 166
Patterson, Stephen J., 36–37, 49
Paul, Saint
  anthropocentric focus of, 33
  atonement theories as
    overlaying readings of, 31
  on basic ecclesial communities,
    50, 57–58, 95, 129, 183–84
  cosmic context to
    understanding of sin, 32
  death and resurrection of
    Jesus, influencing perception
    of, 87
  on death as caused by Adam's
    fall from grace, 14
  on death as the consequence
    of sin, 83
  endtimes, expecting during his
    lifetime, 58, 129, 193
  on fall and redemption as
    going together, 30
  Greek term *sarx,* favoring over
    Hebrew *basar,* 122
  growth, perceiving as a
    consequence of sin, 144
  Jesus, portraying as a rescuer,
    34
  paradox in the works of, 82
  on resurrection as an
    archetypal state of
    deliverance, 40
  on salvation through the
    power of the cross, 38
Pentecostalism, 29, 146

Pereira, Ryan Terrence, 131
Periculoso decree, 56
Phipps, Carter, 145, 161
Pius V, Pope, 56
Pius XII, Pope, 5, 6
Planck, Max, 114–15, 116, 148,
  189
Plato, 1, 133
Popper, Karl, 147
postcolonialism, 7–9, 63, 68,
  100, 176–80
Prigogine, Ilya, 153
printing press link to legalism,
  65–66
Progressive Christianity (PC)
  Center for Progressive
    Christianity, 60
  evolutionary perspective, 63
  focus of, 69–70
  main tenets, 61–62
  as a reconfiguration of the
    faith community, 67–68
  sin and salvation, not
    emphasizing, 64
  as a spiritual bridge, 70–71
Protestantism, 52, 65, 66

quantum mechanics, 10, 12,
  100, 108, 110, 113, 189
quantum vacuum. *See* creative
  vacuum

Rahner, Karl, ix, 164
Raven, Peter H., 144
recapitulation process, 20
reductionism, 22, 42, 95, 120,
  201
relational anthropology, 157
relational identity, 171
relativism, 62, 97, 163, 176
Renaissance era, 66
the residue concept, 8, 177
reworking the tradition, 20, 64, 75

Ricoeur, Paul, 83
Rifkin, Jeremy, 133
Rohr, Richard, 11, 18

sarx (alienation from God), 122
satisfaction theory, 31
Schafer, Lothar, 101, 173
scholastic methodology, 16, 60, 134, 147, 150, 157
Second Vatican Council, 137
Service, Steven R., 105–106
Seung, Sebastian, 154
sexuality, power of, 135–39
Sheehan, Thomas, 179
Shults, F. LeRon, 166
The Sixth Extinction (Leakey/ Lewin), 84–85
Smith, Adam, 86
sophiology, 34
Spirit-Energy-Creation-Evolution-Incarnation-Spirituality, xi, 198
Spong, John Shelby, 49, 64
Stengers, Isabelle, 153
Stewart, John, 152
string theory, 113–14
subjectivity-as-encounter concept, 171
supergravity, 113
survival of the fittest, 96, 142, 144, 152, 153, 155
Swimme, Brian, 10, 80, 110
symbiogenesis, 153

Taylor, Steve, 27
Teilhard de Chardin, Pierre, 143, 145
theology
    Aristotelian anthropology, allegiance to, 172
    comparative theology, 7, 164, 174

cosmic perspective of the new theology, 74
    discernment as primary theological guide, 75
    evolutionary perspective approach, 155–56
    as faith seeking understanding, 4–6
    global theology as an emerging trend, 173–74
    Holy Spirit, theological focus on, 147–48
    inherited theological paradigm, 2
    lay theologians, increase in, 55
    liberation theology, 59, 60
    mainline theological view of Jesus, 156
    placement shift of Jesus in new theology, 160, 163
    priest-theologians, 65–66, 67
    process theology, 16–18, 103
    quantum theory, integrating into theology, 100
    as queen of the sciences, 1, 7
    spirituality, reconciling with, 191–94, 194–97
    theological template of revelation, 3–4
    theology old and new, 15–18
theopoetics, x, 200
theory of evolution, 142
Thomas Aquinas, Saint, 4, 24, 52, 134, 137, 156
three-tier universe, 188, 192–93
Tillich, Paul, ix, 15, 74
torsion waves, 109
Tracy, David, 165–66
Trinity
    essential relatedness of, 117
    ethic of reciprocity and, 63
    in evolutionary context, 158–64

Trinity *(continued)*
    primacy of Christ within, 165
    primordial relationality of the
        Godhead, 138
    reconfiguring understandings
        of, 19
    relationality within, 94

the uncertainty principle, 12

Weinberg, Steven, 155
Wheeler, John, 109
White, Lynn, Jr., 44
Whitehead, Alfred North, 16,
    103
Winter, Miriam Therese, 12, 100,
    107
Witten, Edward, 113
Wright, N. T., 11, 33

zero-point energy, 105